RAGING BEAUTY

RAGING BEAUTY

Selected Poems

James Scully

Azul Editions
MCMXCIV

Published by
Azul Editions
2032 Belmont Rd., N.W.
Suite 301
Washington, D.C. 20009
USA

The Quechua folksongs were co-translated
with Maria A. Proser

Front cover: watercolor / oil marker / eucalyptus leaf
collage by Deirdre Scully

Back cover photo: Museo de Bellas Artes,
Santiago de Chile 1973

ISBN 0-9632363-7-7
Library of Congress Catalog Number: 94-70863

Printed in the United States of America

First Edition
10 9 8 7 6 5 4 3 2 1

CONTENTS

from THE MARCHES (1967)

Facing Up 12
Crew Practice 13
I Frammenti 15

from AVENUE OF THE AMERICAS (1971)

The Field 20
Bartók 21
To Arlene 23
Dead Letter 24
Avenue Of The Americas 33
Dropping Out 38
A Jewish Graveyard Near Leningrad *(translation)* 40
Fish In Winter *(translation)* 42
Walking With Deirdre 44

from SCRAP BOOK (1977)

Winter Journal 46
Treason Of The Clerks 47
North End 53
Seize The Day 54
Poor. Paradise. 57
Paradise 58
With Awful Luck *(translation)* 59

from SANTIAGO POEMS (1975)

When The People Went Extinct 62
Mummies 63
Now Sing 66
Toque de Queda 67
Fascist Pastoral 68
The Day Of The Night 69
Raging Beauty 71
Isa Mar 74
Guerrilla 81

from SCRAP BOOK (1977)

Elementary School 84
Innocence 85
Halfway Into Paradise 88
What Are These *(translation)* 90
Beauty Parlor *(translation)* 92
In Cuzco 94
American Love 96
What Cloud Is That Cloud *(translation)* 97
Fist And Letter *(translation)* 98

from MAY DAY (1980)

Esperanza 100
Angel In Flames 104
Comrade Love 106
Cold Rags 107
Enough! 108
In The Decadence Of Eternity 110
Revolutionary Poetic 112

Frankie Reyes' Poem 115
Bondage, Betrayal 119
Pizza 120
Sandwich Of The Day 121
Motown 122
What Started This *(uncollected)* 124
If *(uncollected)* 125
Socialist Realism 128
As For The Petty Bourgeoisie *(uncollected)* 130
Kurt R 131
Witness César Vallejo 134
Workers United 137

from APOLLO HELMET (1983)

Apollo Helmet 142
Nature Study 145
Capital Punishment *(uncollected)* 147
Pathetic Fallacy 149
Winning The Moral Battle 151
Poverty Is A Bloodbath *(uncollected)* 152
They Glorify Non-Violence *(uncollected)* 153
Poetic Diction 155
Against The Wall *(uncollected)* 157
Revolver 159
The Last Supper 161
The Soviet Union Invades Afghanistan 164
From The Ashes 169
State Power 175
Golden Mean 177
Familiar Terms 178
What Is Poetry 180
Auto-da-Fé *(uncollected)* 183
Poe Votes 184

Flaming A (*uncollected*) 185
The Shameful Dream *(uncollected)* 187
The Sack Of Poetry *(uncollected)* 189
"Our God, Our Help In Ages Past" *(uncollected)* 190
TKO 193
What Are We Waiting For 194
Rhododendron 196

Afterword: Culture War 201

Notes 217

Selected Bibliography 219

For Arlene
John & Deirdre

from THE MARCHES (1967)

FACING UP

A croak out of the marsh in the dark hollow,
drowned chord roaming.
It broke into our sleep.

Then
this March morning, plopped in the dooryard —
that old familiar amphibian

marooned on the crabgrass (a more rugged green)
unmoving, and bigger than life
being blurted out.

Unbeautiful
who turned up, perhaps, for air.

. . . It is the Frog Prince
under a spell of wishing, just under
a cold archaic smile

having come so far, in mottled skin
green and darker green
like dappled leaf, sick, bewitched,

through shades, through clammy depth
coming to be kissed

CREW PRACTICE

for my son, John
Lake Bled, in Jugoslavia

I'd wave the gnats away and try
to tell you, *no one is more dear*,
unable to tell, or think why

and justify our life besides,
hardly in touch. As like that shell's,
fanning water, our shadow glides

down to the dark bottom, beneath
consideration nearly . . . Past
the feudal castle, with each breath

striding much like a galley, or
a leggy water bug, men drop
airs, ages lost in the Great War,

the Austro-Hungarian Empire
and pine island astern — where still
an alpine church upholds its spire

but holds it, also, upside-down
in the water mirror, as though
gravity dragged images down

and drained them off. So many lives.
Caretakers raking the far shore
burn off a winter of wet leaves,

the column of smoke leans. Swallows
blow over all day, worrying
sunset — like quick following harrows

until the sky yields. In widening rings
they orbit, then come back as bats
stroking raggedly on damp wings

(as will the dark, frantic for more,
beat circles over the lamplit
footpath, still darker than before)

equipment in perfect order.

Whenever overtaken, I
duck, nor trust anyone's radar,

not even theirs. Then, when I look
at what comes true, or listen, hard
by the flat tension of a lake

while gooseflesh rises, recalling
how the coxswain's regular bark
marked time, forced rising and falling,

or out of habit dream on Proust,
how little we know or love, those
we know the best and love the most,

then, man to man, this heartless view
tempts me almost to tell a lie,
and wish you better than I do.

I FRAMMENTI

In Memory of Stipin Juričić,
his family & their hospitality
Brela, Dalmacija

1.
Snapshot

Stipin at 74
still poses
paterfamilias stiff
in lavender light

having his picture snapped.
Badly mended
cracked spectacles
gravitate down his nose.

Up the smudged backsliding folds of road
serpentina, a woman tugs
a fat bladdered goat
who hobbles through the dust

an avalanche of pebbles
dragged out at the heels . . .
Stipin's wife.
Unprobed, cancer

mushrooms in her voluminous black blouse, under
the mound of dry goods,
no disaster
but the fact of life.

Beyond all that,
buoyant
on homemade wine and pride
the old man will wave good-bye

babbling broken Italian:
Quan ritorn tu
saro nel
Paradiso.

2.
Memento Mori

Coastal hills
volleyed cuckoo echoes.
They backed us up. They
cut us off from the interior.

The covering of pine trees
the fragrancy
died
down along the beach.

Hollow
hoarse
a jackass hee-hawed
airing the dry heaves.

Raked-over shingle
rattled into the Adriatic
quietly clapping its bones.
No matter

what stones we scaled
how flat
how many times
they dropped out of sight.

Even the washed up sea urchin,
a raspberry-speckled egg
shocked with spines
like a contact mine

crumbled,
powdering our palms . . .
Islands
flourished offshore

virtual Hesperides,
and the miniature
motor driven ferry
running out like a series of duds

touched back and forth, and forth,
suddenly snuffed,
so undependable
we could depend on it.

3.
"UN COUP DE DÉS"

Night, night. Stipin
fiddles with short wave radio
tuned in
to news from over the water.

Out for a breath of air
among the pines' antennae
I clear my head.
Both up and down

the scattered, vaguely whited houses
lodge at a tilt
like chunks off the moon
coming to this,

no village
but a settlement,
where the lime-riddled stone roofs
hold up

as if by pure luck
or less,
a throw of highlights
on the heavily wooded rise.

from AVENUE OF THE AMERICAS (1971)

THE FIELD

for Tomislav Španje,
Brela, Dalmacija

'On the island, in War,
a band of this Partisans
shoot a German patrol.
Next day other Germans
see the dead. And see more —
8 peasants in the field.
And kill all them, the whole
lot. And they go away.
And Partisans go way.
The bodies in the field.'

For each one in the field
a seed. For each, a bullet.
For each one — who stood for
whatever he could get.
And justice for the field,
the sun, the rain . . . the glance
caught out in a downpour
when one man took his wife
or took a cousin's wife
because he saw his chance.

BARTÓK

A man with laryngitis tries to sing
nearly succeeding:

the last quartet. This
is an epic for dwarfs —

who march under
a mercenary liberator

and will not hold their peace
their tongues . . .
                    Hopelessly visionary

crampons in the clutch.
An uprising

whose bodies
depend on murderous charms

of gold and silver, rings and earrings
the ear pierced, the finger

pudgier than ever
garrotted by the ring.

Entranced.
            If prospects
breathe an air of bravery,

if sweetness and grandeur live —
the Grand Canyon's still an abyss.

As who should profess
wisdom — hard on the heels

of so little information,
these pebbles concluding in an avalanche!

TO ARLENE

In your eyes of Pole and Yankee and Jew
        our homeland bleeds
and the night air —

Pack the bags
button up the children

We'll leave.

I'll love you
as Nike loves the mad rush into nowhere
        headless and wingd —

Over Berkeley: choppers
        lullaby
spraying the campus with gas.

In a Middlefield swamp: icepickt, scalded, shot
a black undercover agent
        or patsy
Where is the line to be drawn

Darling
your thighs are fresher than the broom's
        yellow flowers

To be lost in so many thickets —

Domesticity plunges into poetry
        more dear
with the madness coming over this sad land

and against your cheeks
and through your hair

DEAD LETTER

'In high school citizenship I got A
But I knew justice, like poverty,
is irrelevant to poetic legislation
When I'm president
I'll electrocute everyone who is not a
Poet.
And then go into exile seeking
new friends
Who will die for beauty.'
— Grandin Conover

As for the poetry —
it works wonders like a space agency
and saves no one.
Not even poets.
Although at times you called it
an epiphany, or beauty
Singing so assured
it becomes the Coronation Mass,
you also felt poetry
was a cry for help.
While you lived I thought
it *was* the help.
Hardly an answer to human prayer
but like a snakeroot oil
somehow it worked.
It spared me
ulcers, madness
secretive acids were mastered.
And you were poor but never so well off
scribbling in your room.
I believed that.

Graced with a good day I felt
        it was being
completely in touch.
Felt it
        riding out the groundswell
arriving safe on the shore.
Now, I'm not so sure.

Was Shelley an absolute fool?
His poet legislators issue poems
        like a Melanesian congress
producing laws.
Allowed to amuse themselves with advisory power
        they play around, utterly free
to enact a better future.
Meeting once in extraordinary session
        they banned a typhoon. How
enchanted you were, hearing it
What's more the storm
        veered off
and vanished in the Pacific!
(But then, as Shelley knew, the exception
        is merely unusual.
Either that . . . or we'd have to conclude
Melanesia is pure poetry
        along with its wind and rain,
along with what cargo ship what air
transport
        from Jesus from the
        angels
comes in due course like a miracle
touching on thousands, leaving
        foreigners packed and gone
the people happy ever after!)
Well forget it.

Melanesia notwithstanding
no legislator ever dreamed of planning
        a housing project or a social revolution
on lines laid down by Shelley.
Not even the poet himself
        was that kind of fool.
He knew poverty and justice
        as well as he knew
the wind and the water.
He knew the little, or the nothing, he could do.

So did you, except for a few
        delusions of grandeur
and they were called for.
        Maybe that's what poetry is, one of the species
claiming grandeur.
It's that helpless.
Like cockroaches in Florida
        so gorgeous and huge
my landlord called them palmetto bugs.
I crushed them all the same
        oblivious to beautiful
distinctions —
aside from the willingness to kill, quite
        unlike you.
I knew a cockroach
        is a Yahoo.
It stinks. It spoils
        a hundred times more than it eats it secretes
        oils that salve
nobody's wounds.
Killing it's easy
        once you've mastered the technique.
I'm not fastidious, I did it on principle.
Why propose
an extermination program like an exclusive club
        blackballing palmetto bugs
or poets.

What's good enough for cockroaches and people
is swallowed by us.

But then cockroaches are another species
I keep telling myself
like cats, dogs, bushes, bacteria.
Everyone draws the line somewhere.
I could understand Arab herdsmen beating their horses
the way women used to beat dust out of rugs.
Myself I eat meat and wear leather shoes.
Three months already in fall
I survive you.
Who cares how beasts are eaten or killed
as long as men enlightened love themselves.
What rancher was ever that brutal
he christened his cattle
Butchers are also small and wise
like analytic philosophers
they cut everything down to size.
Except themselves.
Keep it in the family though
killing isn't easy, it's murder, it's the species
committing suicide.

Damn it Grandin!
When people used to tell me 'Poets are people'
I thought they were putting down poets
or special pleading
like saying 'We all have a bit of the poet in us.'
But now
(Conjuring a poem, you said
'Every man has the right to think himself extraordinary.'
Delusions of grandeur
or sorcery? I don't know.
In poetry I suppose like voodoo
any man may be a murderer, later
dying of self hatred.)

Your landlady says you were naked
        slumped over your typewriter
sockets pulled out all over the room.
You always refused to submit.
I salute that.
        And always New York
writhed with electrifying connections
like shock therapy or divine light wiping your precious
                                                  human dignity out.
As if you or any man were fit
        to be a specimen
or object.
As though any man able and willing to murder
        even kill himself
parading through the Village conceiving Nietzsche
should twitch like frogs legs
        under the eyes of medical students!
Grandin, it's so
        mundane and painful
like finding Macbeth under a rock.

We're that helpless.
Any child knows as much.
Come night John Grandin drags his feet
        he won't sleep without a story.
I tell about Mario and Gina making
        dangerous journeys in their dreams.
While Pizarro's soldiers ransack the palace
        an Inca herdsman
hurries them up the dark mountainside
to sleep and wait, freezing at the summit
        until the sun rising
throbbing on their faces
        wakes them
safe at home in their own bed.
Becoming once
        a full grown timber wolf
they were shot stealing sheep.

But as it happens
the hot blood cooling waking them
is only urine.
Stinking wet they get up
once again
Mario and Gina.
The story works!
All the fur's gone.
John falls asleep.
Alone I suspect
It's not the story he loves, but some
creature comfort in the telling
snuggling up
his father's body feeling
to him
warmer and stronger than it is.

Three months ago ranging
dangerously over the world, dreaming Australia,
you were young enough to surf.
I thought of you
almost as a son, writing home
plotting exile on exile
like a vision of pure atomic energy.
I took you at your word
the sea and the stars were so beautiful
awful and sure.
Of course it was what
you shouted at the shore
before going under.
Looking back I see
it was just poetry.

I've lost faith in it
but here's a story
just for you.

Imagine a father sitting like a stone in his car
        smoking, reading the newspaper
while his wife shops in the supermarket.
When he looks into the backseat
        the baby's still there
not breathing.
He prods it.
He pinches its nose, breathes
        mouth to mouth lightly
afraid the lungs will burst.
And you know what?
It doesn't matter.
He's left holding
        nothing, which is limp and warm
tasting sour milk on his lips,
what some people call 'the smell of carnations.'
Years after he'll tiptoe
        upstairs listening, straining
to hear the other children breathe.
Such moments he could fall down and worship asthma.
Anything but run dodging cars in the parking lot
        again with his dead son, crying
'she's dead she's dead'
        unable to say 'he.'
Grandin, that man would kill himself
        just to hear it sneeze.
You understand?
        I wonder.
Sometimes I even
poke them to stir them up.
And when in their sleep
        they sigh
the air is munificent as angels
over an empty grave.

Grandin
the most callow cocksucker on Macdougal St.
where every evening's
mardi gras in the 21st century
has sweeter breath than you
left down there in that sandlot
on the Jersey shore.

Once in a poem I called you a frog
Frog Prince really
coming to be kissed.
What I never mentioned was . . .
That day you kissed me on the forehead
instead of me you
I committed you.
Not so strangely, nothing changed.
Under the mutilating calm of needles and pills
you held your breath,
got time off for good behavior
the way rats get pellets, obeying rules
so arbitrary they're unquestionable.
You pretended
doing what you had to do.
And I though never a princess or god or plain
good friend saving your life —
I have no regrets.
No more than you.
Epiphanies like poetry seldom come
shining as we expect.
Under conditions that would have crushed any godforsaken
prince
you managed to hold up croaking and singing
braver than most men.

Jim Hall says they should have dumped your body in the
streets of New York
and left it there
That would be a monument.
Meanwhile the rest of us survive
dreaming of poetry
as madmen dream they'll die in Jerusalem.
Only poetry's
hard on them, and children die of it
the older they get.
They're not up to it
the way friends or lovers are hardly ever
in tune with friendship or love.
Even the beautiful are too
heartsick for beauty,
astronauts will never make it to the stars
but burn up.
Justice
is equally murderous
dear Grandin.
Like poetry, poverty, like
a most unhappy life —
take even a poet
or any man. He is not up to it.

AVENUE OF THE AMERICAS

Back towards Sixth Avenue
        at 3 a.m. . . . with you
musing, padding along the concrete.
Without
        warning you flash out, disconnected
as a news bulletin:
        'This is it
the most degenerate part of the city.'
                                        'Why? What's . . .'
        'Because
it's the Avenue of the Americas.'

In a week I'll phone you
Police will answer, not pigs
but something human
        intoning: 'I'm sorry. I don't know.
I didn't find him.
You must feel
        They just left me
to watch the body.'

Tonight though
you show me
        your seedy haunts.
So they won't be lost

Bars are air-conditioned
caves.
At the International you call attention
to the walls —
shirtless cowboys, heroically drawn
        steel workers pouring
molten steel.

Socialist Realism? You wonder at
        the proletarian ideal.
The studs-and-leather crowd mixes it up,
bruisers
        huddle, making love.
The way they look, they might have stepped
        off the walls
into this hole
An oldtime communist bar
for workingmen.
You raise the question, 'Is this
        what the 30s have come to?
Or was it, even then
what that scene was all about?'

We slip out.

Some hangout by the docks, we're thrown
back to the 50s.
It's like high school.
        One pool shooting dude
plays at Viking, hair swept back
        like deep swells at sea,
striking goatee . . .
He doesn't make it.

Wellbuilt derelicts post
        themselves at corners.
Each with his doorway, storefront, or leans
        one foot cocked back
against an iron picket.
Scouting the sidewalk
        for a pick-up, it's
themselves they ignore!
You can't
        figure them out.
'Not even by sleeping with them'
you say

We glide by
        out of reach
as a tourist and his guide.

At the White Horse having left
Jim and his girl
Agreed she's no less
intelligent than beautiful . . .

Night before, you'd dreamed
    you married Jackie Onassis
She scrubbed your back in the bathtub
her knees dug at your skin.
    A little man in dark glasses
you kept begging her to let you in . . .

And we'd
Agreed, too, next time I visit
    to pick up
a couple of eastside chicks
and spend lots of money . . .
Camaraderie.

At dinner we'd talked of Vallejo
    and winced
poor bastard,
collecting bottles for his bread.

Later I threatened
'you won't get away with
    "Proposals for a New Society"
I'm writing a reply.'

You laughed
    amused
and, I think, happy.
You could dig that.

. . . Suddenly I'm in a cab.
You're standing in the avenue
Neon pallor, like a terrible psychedelic poster
        saying something
I don't understand.

You reach in the window to shake hands.
In 10 years we have never, even,
        shaken hands.
Now. I cannot understand.

The cab takes off. You step back
Your last words
sear,
        a parting shot:
'You know I've always adored you.'

'Dig it Grandin' I
        toss back, abstracted
as if I hadn't really heard.
Lighting a cigarette, scared
Trying to brush your words off
        like hot sparks.
My shirt will burn.
My ship

I never bargained for this.

'E. 67th' I tell the cabbie
once more,
rounding a corner.

Speed
        eases me
back into the seat.
I'm fugitive. The window's open
        on all that

dying out behind me, downtown . . .

You're saying
'You know, I always adored you.'

Yes, I know.

DROPPING OUT

'It is impossible to live in a society
and to be free of that society.'
— Lenin

Twenty years ago, witch hunt meant congressional subpoena:
slap with a paper glove. Now it may be a shotgun.

And no one's career is ruined anymore,
because career is an obsolete word.

To get up and go to work is pushing genocide
the poor and intelligent say —

although the worst hasn't yet come true
except in principle.

Today, paranoia. Tomorrow, Delmore Schwartz back from the
grave, saying
even paranoids have enemies.

Rumors clutter the kitchen table
like bomb threats piling up in public telephones.

The question is not if or whether
but when and how.

In your heart, you've begun to weigh moral distinctions
between one murder and another,

your heart sinks
to the level of a court of law.

Around you, successful men swallow what's left of their pride
as others overdose on pleasant drugs, intending suicide.

Behind you, your childhood is littered with truths
you thought anyone would die for —

like the leaves this fall, the wretched yellowing
of white shirts no one bothers to wear.

No more the blazing, breathless
redgold of a sudden cold snap!

Leave?

Wherever a man might step, it seems
he put his foot down on someone's head.

'A JEWISH GRAVEYARD NEAR LENINGRAD'

A Jewish graveyard near Leningrad.
A crooked fence of rotting plywood.
Behind the crooked fence they lie, side by side,
lawyers, shopkeepers, musicians, revolutionaries.

For themselves they were singing.
For themselves they were saving up.
For others, they were dying.
But first they paid taxes,
                    deferential to the collector,
and in this world, desperately material,
interpreted the Talmud,
                    remaining idealists.

Maybe they saw . . . more.
Maybe, they believed blindly.
Yet they taught their children to accept
and to hold out.
And they did not sow the wheat.
                    They never sowed wheat.
Only, they were laying themselves down
in the cold earth, like seeds.
And were falling asleep forever.
And later, earth was being scattered over them
and candles were lighted,
and on the Day of Atonement
hungry old men, their high voices
pinched with the cold, cried out for peace.

And they were finding it.
                    In the breakdown of brute matter.

Nothing, no remembering.
Nothing, no forgetting.

Behind the crooked fence of rotting plywood,
within four kilometres of the trolley turnaround.

(Joseph Brodsky, Russia)

FISH IN WINTER

Fish live in winter.
Fish nibble oxygen.
Fish swim in winter,
grazing their eyes against
                                        ice.

There.
        Where it's deeper.
Where the sea is.

Fish.
        Fish.
                Fish.

Fish swim in winter.
Fish want to swim out.
Fish swim without light,
under a sun orb
                        wintry and shaken.

Fish swim away from death.
Ever. That is the way
                            of fish.

Fish do not shed tears,
stiffening their heads against
                                        the bluffs of ice.

            In cold water
            the cold eyes
              of a fish
               freeze.

Fish are silent, always.
For they're —
dumbstruck.

Rimes about fish,
like fish,
stick in my throat.

(Joseph Brodsky, Russia)

WALKING WITH DEIRDRE

That rush you thought was river water —
            it was spring
clearing over the boulders.

                                        Once, from underfoot
a ruffed grouse flew up like a terrified heartbeat . . .

To open a window
— Pasternak observed this
            before he melted into the landscape —
is to open a vein.

Walking with you
                            opens a door.
Flushed, it's glorious, what is there more?

I stand here, cold as the mountains
            the March sun began to warm
and water trickles
                            running out of the rock.

Deirdre, bountiful daughter, we'll never die out.

from SCRAP BOOK (1977)

WINTER JOURNAL

I'd sat alone in the Sistine Chapel
as in an old barn

So bone creeping cold
even the guards had gone.

Against the Judgment wall Michelangelo crumpled
his own skin like a trophy

Adam, waking, had already dreamed the God
rather than face himself . . .

What went wrong? that we'd got up to make
a masterpiece of our misery.

The sky, if it had feeling, would also grow old
wrote Chairman Mao.

The guards, they guarded a stove in the storage room
thawing their fingers and toes.

THE TREASON OF THE CLERKS

Our blood rose
as sap through a system,
Like the civil service of Chinese men of letters
working their way up.

A few of course refused
to live by the rules.
Grandin skipped class, holed-up writing
As The Hawk Sees It
His only set, the U.S. Embassy
shook like a future refugee: Berlin 1936
as the hawks seized it.
When the manuscript was stolen
with a suitcase full of clothes
He went ragged, wrote another year.
That finished his career.
All he found written in his book
was treason
Graffiti like
'Art and Science are your only seasons
Pray use them as switchblades, like a poet,
not as wallets or semesters.'

And Tu Fu failed the Imperial examinations
twice.
The establishment . . . his best
poetic prose couldn't get him in.
Grandin couldn't pass
an I.Q. test for the draft
He fell asleep instead.
And took off for parts unknown
again again

Nine years later, the chief medical examiner
City of New York
forwarded his opened letter.
The message?
'The unquestioned
is the only answer there is.'

Nevertheless
Neil and I among others
passed with flying colors
We were
a heartwarming disgrace
like conscripted soldiers who have won a war.
When he inscribed *The Dream That Was No More A Dream*
(about the Third Reich
as theatre come to life)
Neil called it his coloring book.
Graduated into a think tank
He tried to breathe
ethics into computers
humanism into universities.
Which took like a vaccine.
They were immune.
Daemonic
he designed and rehearsed a scenario
— Totalitarian Classroom —
so true to life
it was like getting an education.

What I did
was higher learning.
Was paid to do it, to people
who could pay to have it done.
Public education
it didn't cost much,
Just enough to keep the dirt
poor out.

Those who were well-off wore privilege
like fatted calves
They had everything
anyone would think to have.
The best of them
tossed and turned
Like Adam, dreaming he would share
the awful windfall of Eden

Only
the years pass.
The day came
I sat among the students, refused to speak
5 minutes, 10 —
Across the room
a girl I thought I knew
screamed
'What do you want us to do!'

It's cold mornings,
I get up
it's another age.
I'm at court, a tutor
spanking the princes who could make him eat grass
— no not princes
pillows stuffed with insurance.
Beautiful
boys and girls
they smile, spoiled.
Why should they be so complacent, so bruised
sitting there.
I talk down
pouring out words: for ruined children
the future of the middle class.

Jayne above all . . .
Rainy days
            her hair
sprang ringlets to show Dante the light
                              the mere glimmer of it
Held in a classroom where the windows had gotten dark,
            whole semesters gone up in cigarette smoke,
She wanted this
            lecture parading as discussion
conducted outside.
Spring
        spring before
She'd had a Sociology class
                                    out in the apple orchard
'Petals were falling
            all over us
on our heads and shoulders
between the pages of our books . . .'

I would go anywhere with her.

I didn't turn a hair.

Already the night air smacks of fall
Each weekend the flurry of parties
            piles up, thicker and more brilliant.
Strange. When Tu Fu got the censor's job, even then
            his children starved.
How many?
Chronicles won't say.
Our lives as leaves grow
                        glorious sickening on the sugar maples,
First light touch of spring
            pails cling to them
greedy, draining the sweet.

And his last job, adviser to a petty warlord in Szechuan
well after the An Lu-shan rebellion
        he drifted away from.
Under the cold stars, the same
        Tu Fu who once shared a blanket with Li Po
as though they were brothers.
He went down the Yangtze.
He might be a log
        except for the poetry,
With different versions of his death
passed down
            by word of mouth.
And of his family, nothing more is heard . . .

This mouth would move
        once, only when it wished.
Three winters
        in the summer cottages, we shivered
by a kerosene stove.
We were green students.
4 a.m. one night
        Neil walked across the frozen lake
just to talk.

Now he jets
            clear over the Atlantic
Only they pay him
        to keep talking.
They pay me as well.
Having had
            misfortune to pass the exams
Tu Fu had the misfortune
to fail.

Today a Russian woman asked
            'Where's your intelligentsia?'
I say, mine is yours
All times
        everywhere.
We give cold comfort to one another
like evergreens in headlong
   gusts of rain
        loaded with snow dripping down,
like whippoorwills sounding the night.

Neil, old distant friend
        more bird of feather than friend —
And Tu Fu whose brush strokes
        bleeding out each bud, leaf, cumulus
                    rose to meet the elements —
And that other friend
        mounting the western imagination, inviting me
O to fly away —
                    the beauty is,
between this earth and that sky
we owed nothing to no one,
   All along
          green as needles, shoulder by shoulder
with everything that lives,
we were paying our way with our lives

NORTH END

Hartford, Connecticut
16 years old, two children
struggling alone

Peaches, I tell it cold as I can.
That winter's morning you stared out the window
into the filthy
wind
the honey colored slum
you said, as though saying nothing

'when I wake up in the morning
I don't want to wake up'

SEIZE THE DAY

Women I had
like swatting houseflies.
Men know what that meant
Knocking off a piece

Screwing it to death
I came
I saw stars.
There wasn't a soul around.

Nights were pure murder
like slumming, 5 banged her out in the car
One bitch I robbed.
Drunk as lords
we dropped bills all over the black-&-tan bars,
Money the ultimate muscle.
We figured that much.
Brain matter mixed with leaves, that color
Dollars
anyone can smell the perfume of
drugged them to their knees,
Subtler than the swish of aerial whips . . .
The way Aztec warriors used to mill about
singing flower wars
To kill with flowers

I danced my ass off
into the small hours.
High, in concert we
stomped a guy to the floor.
Terror.
And taking off, peeling rubber, fired
Twice, missed!

Shadows rushing out
                                        froze.
It was a nightmare,
no one got hurt.

It was night all day.
Balls chafed
          young and sore
a gang dragging through the city,
Whoever got away?
Cock erect
          like an insomniac,
no future in that.
We lived though
          like there was no tomorrow

I never knew sorrow.

I sang with the cats
Here pussy here
          pussy pussy pussy fur
the way a jet screamed over sopping jungle
          throttling it
To no end.
There was none
          only surroundings.
Dusk glared all night
          down the violet lighted avenues, even
Greenery swallowed
          all we drove into it.
Spunk, rubbers, junked cars aflame
forgotten as last month's clap, drip, hot . . .
          we were
amnesic as pain
the night after
the night

My god like a scar
                feeling nothing
I was ecstatic.
I gave it all I had

POOR. PARADISE.

Coming at last
into our own land,
we were
where we are

Alone together in another slum,
bristling
          like cactus glory in the desert,
We too
          erect were bliss
We wished only for what is.
My heart was in your mouth
Blood under your skin was juice
          easing my lips
Our word came forth naked
courting what is.
What is
          blessed us, blessing enough for us.

One human being was no human being.

In our tribe everyone starved
or no one did

PARADISE

There are no men, no women,
there is human

Without irony,
because what's left to wish for

Making love is more
than poor stick buried in a hole.

Finger-tips dance over buttocks and breast
as ants through the fresh-turned earth

So thoroughly into life
we need not describe it anymore

WITH AWFUL LUCK

With awful luck, pained we saw our pain.

Broken lances
lie in the roads,
hairs are scattered about.
The houses are roofless,
their walls hot
red hot.
Worms sprout through the streets and plazas,
the walls are flecked with brains.
Waters are red, red as if dyed,
and if we drank
it was saltpetred water.
TERRIFIED WE BEAT AT THE MUD WALLS
and we were left with our heritage:
a net of holes.
We put our lives behind our shields,
but shields do not hold off
the desolation.
We have eaten crumbs of bird seed,
we have chewed bitter dog grass,
adobe chips, small lizards, mice
and ground up earth and even worms . . .

(Aztec, c. 1521/28)

from SANTIAGO POEMS (1975)

WHEN THE PEOPLE WENT EXTINCT

Santiago de Chile, 12.X.73

And when the people went extinct
they left the blue roof of their monument
to rot in peace

And not a soul left in sight
except Neruda, dying of cancer
under house arrest

And not a stick of furniture, but one
bloody sofa
which was christened 'Allende'

And when the dream graffiti of the poor
had left the cornerstones, the river banks
filthy bright with beauty

— and after all that
had been wiped out —
the mummies came back to light, unwinding

their glad rags through the streets: the desolate
chic
of Providencia in spring

It was nothing to cry over.

MUMMIES

Because all the forces at our command
invaded our constitution

we lived in a foreign country,
we called it Chile

Because we had a ballot, because our bodyguard
pumped bullets into it

we were glad
we were scared

Because we attacked our factories
(because they were manned by workers)

we couldn't do an honest day's work

And having burned one Picasso
in the street, we couldn't see right

Because we set Victor Jara up to sing
Venceremos

to murder once and for all
the song in the man

by murdering this man

we lost our voice

and having fired Neruda's
last book of poems

because the plain words on cheap paper
anyone could read

and having put out
the eye of our prose

we were numb all over

Because we pulped 8 newspapers
it was an old story

Because, at the State Technical University, professors
refused to leave their desks

we learned nothing by killing them

but taught some students a lesson
not one remembers

Because we stripped men women and beds
naked in the Hospital of the Saviour

we caught a chill
from which we could not recover

And when the National Stadium raised its colors
as a concentration camp

torture like soccer
became a national sport

Because every morning, more workers' corpses
jammed the trolley terminal, we could get nowhere

Because we fished odds and ends
of bodies from the Mapocho

and dumptrucked the rest
(spoiled) into the Pacific

— bread lines withered,
abundance came back on us

In the style to which
we had been accustomed

again, we were free to live
on our own flesh and blood

NOW SING

NOW sing: the guards howling
beat him with obscenities.
    But he did.
His legend is
He was singing
                    Venceremos
when they shot him.
Even for them, it was too much

they killed him,
they couldn't kill him enough.

Victor Jara
            sin guitarra,
who'd held out with bloody stumps
                                        and sung

TOQUE DE QUEDA

Already the greengrocer's on Merced
is shuttered up.
        Who cares
now, if he charged too much,
or that his thumb worked greasy miracles
                        with scales

What few people are left
            are newspapers the wind blows
over and over. What difference is it
        what lies they told,
what stories
buried

That one, with the bundle tucked under his arm,
he was a child once
        clutching its pillow,
        His head's
                wrencht
over his shoulder, where the fear is

And the fat man with a limp, it's terrible
to see him hurrying!
He was not built for this
        but for an easy chair, a sweet illegal
pastry: of sugar, flour, butter.
But with a hunger
    now
no black market can satisfy,
he drags and is swinging his leg
        as though it were young, gawky and flighty
                        O so wild
as never could get enough out of life

FASCIST PASTORAL

What did you expect: blood?
But blood dries up,
        nights
                come home
like a flock of smudged pastoral poems

Are fairy tales what
        the poor wish?
then pastoral is the propaganda
of the sordid

Running lights out
        helicopter hovers
with its rabbit thump, rabbit thump
        And sharp dull
clatter of shots:
        like planks
slapped down on a lumber stack . . .

But muffled, as a held breath
                all night
mushrooms: a slumridden
        meadow
of raw wood shacks.
                Which at dawn
beg to be burnt to the ground.

LISTEN THERE'S BLOOD, BUT BLOOD ISN'T
THE WORST THING ON EARTH
What is, is people suffering their silence
                like sheep —

who had only aspired to suffer
as human beings

THE DAY OF THE NIGHT

The day of the night
they arrested Fernando:
I'm lounging on a bench,
among retired old men
and purple flowers
in the Plaza de Armas.

A one-legged man
rolls his sleeves up
and hums: over
an iron water bubbler
bubbling over
his hands and forearms.
Having dropped his crutch
he's washing away.
The wornout
blue of his shirt
is gray as the overworked sky.
He could be a cloud
            blue
bird with spindly legs,
standing, one leg
more or less straight,
the other tucked up
under its belly:
tossing a splat of drops
off, onto the packed dirt
under a huge leafy palm
that droops and crests
— but motionless —
in carbon monoxide
it can live with,
the way an oasis
lives with desert.

He will stand
72 hours, without
a thing to eat,
a black
hood over his head.

If we had wings, roots, petals
we would not be men.

RAGING BEAUTY

Having come so far, I find
myself on a streetcorner
                    of North America.
Hair sharked back with water,
blade in pocket:
willing to cut
          anyone's throat,
like 20 years ago.
I never left.

Now in the glass domed
Museo de Bellas Artes
I stare
          like a barbarian
at works of art:
                    at *Bride of the Wind,*
          at *Caryatid,*
the rarified shit
wishful men and women
          end up with,
Who grope for beauty everywhere
but where they are.

The daybright dome is almost
beautiful as sky.
                    It is.
          But what does it sing to itself
                              at nightfall
alone in the dark with its acre of dusty hall,
its few sculptures
like gelded boulders . . .

The river's
spitting distance away. Bridgehead too
I go to --
where a pure heart has painted
bold graffiti:
verses giving birth
to hammer and sickle banners,
Silhouette
heads conceived
bald as slates, but red
yellow white and blue,
As bright and primary
as a nursery.
New as it is
it mildews,
The muddy shallows of the Mapocho
ripple every inch, stopping at nothing

until 20 years have gone by
like a rusty knife . . .

Until I'd give anything
to go away
myself, with the river,
Not now, but someday
free to rage:

'We didn't
diminish what we touched,
we weren't
children forever
we stood ground and grew,
what we made we made
human, with a human face'

standing on this bridge
between the 19th century museum
and 21st graffiti,
between one death and another
while the horrible water runs under

ISA MAR

for Isabel Margarita Letelier

1

What a get-together it was
in the New York restaurant.
When your hair tumbled down
        to your hips,
Pablo went wild over it.
Baptizing you 'Isa Mar'
        — as a dark sweettoothed water
                running over —
he scribbled
        you or her
fugitive verses on napkins.

You were rushing back, into
        the mercurial black
sea syllables of Isa Mar . . .

Isabel Margarita stayed on the shore.

2

                Isabel, what do you hear?
Your husband's marooned: off Tierra del Fuego
        on Isla Dawson.
It's a small world, smaller than the moon
Its tiny fires illumine no one.

Day and night
watchtowers train their sights
into the concentration camp,
others
stare at the sea.
No flushed human face
swims into view.
But welcome
penguins
like ambassadors, who keep their distance.
The Antarctic Circle brims with wildlife,
why is it
it transmits nothing
but waves of cold and wet . . .

No longer under house arrest,
But doing time
in this plush apartment
your eyes widen: globular.
Flesh is heavier
because your heart is.
You could be a page boy
nibbling, waiting for messages,
your hair cut and set.

Behind a TV screen
as in a shadow play
the general gavels his fist.
His captive audience
is 10 million souls.
His office is so close
The polaroid windows
reflect
a feeble brass sunset
down at your window.

When he opens his mouth,
        all Santiago
contracts to a shrunken head

The poet is dead.
                The Ministry of Public Works
lugs his urn, from one rented mausoleum
        to another.
His land can't live with it.
Which tosses and turns
        in the General Cemetery
like a relic thrown into the sea . . .

Isa, in grinding silence
        between one hemisphere and another
the scraps of poems
to you, went under

3

In your purplish dark
        mother-of-pearl look, there's
a cave to curl up in:
                listening
to cold black waters
crashing sidelong at the shore

                        . . . out of which comes
                Pablo
fleeing the hospital, the mummy beds
of Santiago.
He needs
        Isla Negra
to die in.

He loves the brute
semiprecious stones.
Loves what
bursts into life, like birds!
And wants, and gets, a wall cage of creaks and flutters,
an iridescent tapestry
that preens, couples, sings, craps,
whose feathers fly.
He wants the bliss
of dying
where life throbs and is shameless,
because it's the only way to live.
His bed's set
kitty-corner in the room.
He gazes at the sea
going from iris to blue to black, to green
and iris, out through the window . . .

Orlando, too, shows up
odd with his red hair.
When he called his office, who answered
but a general.
He held the phone up in the air:
'Listen
to the voice of a traitor.'
Then ate his breakfast, read the paper,
in utter calm
is driven to prison.
In Dawson
he makes a tin can coffee cup
and well, with a reedlike handle.
Behind barbed wire
he won't be cowed,
and won't
stoop to shout.

Your days and nights
eddy and stream around
this russet rock,
this still standing man.

O but now
Where earth ends, old
General Pinochet
pokes up
his grandfatherly head,
Barking like a seal
out in the mist.
His eyeballs
sting, he can't
sleep, can't see
through the blood web.
And is addicted
to stiff white uniforms
like self-torture,
To recall
how crisp
and clean it used to feel?
What happened to the boy
his mother called
Augusto, Augusto!
What's left
gropes awake in a strange familiar blood

Your black heart heaves and heaves
too deep for hate.
You turn these up
and slip away, saying
live a beautiful life

4

Recall, Isabel, the nights
you plunged in icy water
        over your head —
so young, you and your friends
played as porpoises.
But warmed up
on raw pisco.
That was the life then.

And once a Gypsy took your money.
Cursing her you yanked
        her thick braids
off, they were fake!
You were both so
                shockt
she gave the money back . . .

Isabel, this is for you,
for the cold,
for the lost scraps
        of poems to Isa Mar,
for the rest that won't come back
because it went without saying.

It's true: curlicues of praise
        like ribbons
refuse to be wasted.
If Pablo knew anything at all
this is what he knew.

You're not the wrinkling, stone deaf
          body of salt and water —
but a high spirited, enduring woman.
But a girl, a girl too
who answers to Isabel
                    Isabel Margarita!
No poetry is lost on you.

GUERRILLA

After so many lovely faces
went ashen, too delicate for words

and skittered away
until their backs looked like backs,

we hunkered down
and sang: horribly, but sang.

And when we swallowed, we brooded,
our skin listened

to its own cells, its buried children
giggling in the dark.

And wept for the inch deep brook
stroking its moss, and the swamp

of yellowy woods, sticks with petals,
and the shaggy hump of meadow

glittering with spittlebugs, fizz-drops
brimming their joy to the edge of the wood . . .

Spit on our lips was beautiful
struggling to say love is what it is.

Facing up, up, we found ourselves
in this sorrowful army, the army that wins

by rage and error, and by winning over:
but always, coming only to be kissed.

from SCRAP BOOK (1977)

ELEMENTARY SCHOOL

for Teresa Perez
Santiago de Chile, X.73

Why is it the trivial saying
warbles with rage, and fear.

Shaken. *This is the rain*
that kills the little birds.

She said birds, she meant
children.

And the rain was weapons
inspecting the books,

the rain was dollars, a hush
scudding across the earth

the rain was workers, peasants, it was misery
raining tears, blood, dirt.

What after all was rain
but the lesson —

that birds were children
the wind blew, the rain struck and slurred . . .

until the children learned
they were not children,

nor rain rain,
birds birds

INNOCENCE

Like any brute, to have a soft heart.

To be the last benevolent despot
or revolutionary without arms.

Imprisoned by Bonaparte
to embrace Sade,

to spit out, as he did,
'At least *I* never killed anyone'

To have thought that good
or good enough.

Like any beast, to have dreamed
murder begins or ends

in flesh and blood.

So. To have sought like a dog
panting with peace and love

Or bought a man or woman
however thrilled or willing the ruin

To have used a piece of human.

To didn't mean to do it
and be sincere.

You held yourself pure
regardless.

You thought you were the motto?
You were the money.

And once upheld the Universal Declaration of Human Rights,
forgetting to feed the cat.

A man and woman of principle
a real shit

to have been wishful,
for ever and ever

To have sung your starry ideal
lulling as an alibi

Evening news rocked like a bedtime story

so awful and graceful
it had no moral.

You had been above all
impartial

Every question, like genocide,
had at least two sides

every question a burning answer.

You wept at the blood,
washed and wept

for the good it did.

Bitter at the end,
guilt was your pride and joy

because you were shameless.
You had no sense of shame.

You were no solution.
You were you.

My heart went out to you
as an executioner,

it did what it had to do.

You could not, could not tell
my heart from my hand.

HALFWAY INTO PARADISE

1.

Halfway into Paradise
            Dante hears
the advice he wants to hear:
'Tell the whole truth.
No lies.
If it stabs them
            sick, even to tears
let them pick at their own scabs.'

That's what I say

I say that.

2.

Now I hear
                        a pure spirit or wise guy
put this burning question to Chou En-lai:
Why. Why didn't he
            push the revolution to the hilt
and finish the job.
Chou replied, 'Look here
            look at my mother.
She has bound feet.
What can she do
            but hobble around.
If I cut them loose, she would fall down.'

That's what I say

I say that.

3.

So torn the gut

howls in its pit

WHAT ARE THESE

What are these?
They're senators! that for
a mingey salary
will start a war

Mariano Baptista
the great speechmaker
I stick on the rooftops:
that tightfisted milker

Mendizabalcito
has plunged into the mud
ah! but he's gotten up
all covered with gold

Look at that
senator, look inside him:
nothing! No, but
his pockets are stuffed

The priest of Mizque
has written me, saying:
Senators!? You might as well
cut off their balls

Mendizabalcito
has fallen into the water, ah
but he's gotten out again
dry as a bone

Senators of the valley
can't find their tongue,
because they don't have one
they cultivate their fingernails

Every mother's son
lives on his land, in his house.
Only I, poor exile
have no home no homeland

What Jiménez de Asúa said
is clearer than pure water:
Among our presidents, is where
the biggest thief will be

(Quechua folksong)

BEAUTY PARLOR

Gold
and misery
of Peru. Parlor
of horrors
and beauty. I have said,
seen
and heard, with my soul
clinging to the earth. I see —
being born in blood, the face
of the rose, in night the day, in afternoon a sky
wide open as the carcass of a steer, the gold
pure under the sky of gold.
I see
the sun
being born, the day
dying, daily, in flames,
and this is the same — or almost the same —
as a graveyard of living rot.
And the sea
goes on, the sea rolling round
like a hoop in the sea, the sky
face down, I go on seeing
and hearing
drenched children in the streets, begging
bread
they pay only thank-you for, good-bye for
the misery received.
Everything
muttered, all
disjointed, lying there, broken,
I see
misery coated with smiles, meals
eaten off newspaper, and I hear

the sun from a silent bell
sounding out
against me, against everyone,
for having pointed the poem into the ulcer
the parlor
(of beauty and horror) in which we endure.

(Alejandro Romualdo, Peru)

IN CUZCO

Peru, X.73

Something they had to celebrate,
so came
bundled in ponchos
the sodden color of old copper,
and in alpaca skullcaps
with pom poms
with earflaps curling up ¡ay!
and bare feet, cardboard shoes, in suit jackets
round-shouldered as the cobblestones,
and highdomed panama hats
painted white,
white with a black band,
and in petticoats,
in chemical blue
tennis shoes

a trumpet they had, flutes
beating at skin
drums and a bass drum too,
and placards waved in the dusk: as though
swatting at bats
with wands,
brushing away the Cerro Corporation,
its yanquis, its paper
deeds
rattling their chains in the dark . . .

Dispossessed of all
but original insolence
(the heart in its ribs
like a bloody rag in a fist)

they quick-stepped
through the cold wet street,
hupping and fluttering a red flag

AMERICAN LOVE

Peru, X.73

We did not sacrifice
the human, but had

40 and more
kinds of potatoes,

a few to spread out
on strewn wet grass

these we left: 4, 5 nights
to freeze on the top ridge

and each morning, underfoot
squeezed the moisture out

till they were hard as rocks
and kept for years,

but soaked in warm
water an hour or more

they softened and swole
they made a stew

and no one starved,
we always had food

we never *had* to say
I love you

WHAT CLOUD IS THAT CLOUD

What cloud is that cloud
gathered so close?
Probably my mother's tears
turning to rain.

I'm a man traveling alone,
I have no mother no father,
until even the tree by the road
is a tree that gives no shade.

Bringing me into the world
my mother said: "You will be a man."
And father: "You'll be a worker
and a slave," he said. And wept.

Between this day and the next
I leave on a long journey.
If there's life, I can come back.
If death, not ever again.

Purely by chance, I have a mother
that I may have a father
that he may say, some day:
"Where is my son?"

(Quechua folksong)

FIST & LETTER

Put
the letter
in your fist: Write, write, write
against wind and tide, against shadow,
against this whole horrible masquerade
that passes daily before our eyes.

Put
your fist
in the letter: And blot, blot, blot out
the blood buckling us in, the shadow
spilled across the soul, the terrifying
misery
that peoples the face of charity.
Strike
with the letter.

Put
your mouth
at the bottom
of this pit: And sing, sing, sing
truths you can put in your fist.

(Alejandro Romualdo, Peru)

from MAY DAY (1980)

ESPERANZA

The bony black face
of Esperanza

archaic face
of blood work, chicken
slaughter, pin feathers, salted carcasses,
of hands condemned to glow
in cold dreamless water,
cold cement
stopping the feet dead,

the look of work
and strike, one more
picket with a slag foot rhythm
that says, we won't kill ourselves,
we can walk this line forever,
or what amounts to forever . . .

Esperanza is sick of forever.

On the strict iron
of the fire escape, she bristles
like chilblains in sunlight
resting her bones against the warm brick wall.

Against the world, which is
legal and Anglo, she yanks
a lavender vinyl collar across her face.
Not like an ostrich, but an old opera.
They want her soul her bread
her food stamps, welfare
check, slave pay,
her 30 dollar a week

union dole.
Her man, her coat.
Even at night
she pulls the night over her head.
Even her cunning
gets carried away
on the wings of her innocence.

The cold damp air
is killing her.
She's picking up what she can,
flying back
to Puerto Rico,
wherever it is —

a thin black bird
good morning'd and fed,
have a pleasant trip
as never before, never again,
in the belly lap
of a huge silver bird . . .

coming down into
factory clouds of sunset chemicals,
flecks of ash,
the queasy
blue wrinkled bay water,
skimming and overshooting
rows of stunted
pineapples withering in the field

a few shreds
of fading color,
the same earth
she had come from, gone to, and left.

A swollen superport
rose from the sea, draining the sea.
A third of the women had been sterilized.

Limousines
sped past vacant lots. Gardenias.

A mountain of nickel,
gouged face . . .

Esperanza
shivered to bone
in the throat of restaurants,
in plump bodega hearts,
and in the labyrinth of refineries
— high flying
            torches
                      burning off the night —
in the sublime
filaments of computers
that could not swallow her,
and cannot spit her out.

Now all the hand-slapped guitars
put on
smiles of glass.
They have a mouthful
of sharp dark bird, petty
thievery, acrid
envy;
Esperanza
fills their mouths with blood.

. . . Unborn skies
come to stare: at broken
palm fronds, broken words,
at what seem to be
hands
wrung like flags of shame.

To stare, and wonder how so much
wealth made so much poverty
so much alone,
how so much misery
made Esperanza

who expected
nothing

scavenge in the cracks
of her own hands.
This
thing that existed only

to bury her face in the dust of Puerto Pobre.

ANGEL IN FLAMES

Angel on this broken street
is dressed to the teeth.

He has his dignity.

*

Under the dove gray fedora
there's a wage slave
out of work.

He has his dignity
against a wall.

*

And under
the wasp-waisted shirt,
extravaganza of black volcanic glass
crusht in daisies
ay! there's the merest rib cage,
bird bones of winter,
a sallow angel

*

And in the
quick brown eyes
like worry beads
that cannot read,

and the fingers
with their walking stick,

which is really a weapon
that cannot write —

there is the bonfire of poetry

*

Angel is a slave out of work.

Someday he's going to kill someone.

*

His small hands
have flown at clouds,
sick with blood
with glass
banks shimmering in distance,
the sharp
stink of weed,
stone throat,
star
sapphire
flash and rush of cops . . .

*

Graffiti
choke the street,
blaring off these walls . . .

*

Angel in flames
will blacken the sky

COMRADE LOVE

Your cheekbones,
the last bit of afternoon sky,
are suddenly rose-stained brass.

Down the street
it's night before we know it.

November has raked the trees.
They stick out
awry in the murk: twisted rods
the concrete has crumbled away from.

They are not trees
but fireworks black with frost.

Our boots are ringing, stamping the raw gray
                                        of everything hard . . .

We were bringing the heavens home.
We had married one another
to a bleak, elated planet.

Unconscious of caring, in blind honor
we took this life like an iron bar
— it was frozen —
and still we put our lips to it.

COLD RAGS

Where did everyone go?

Enemies depress the air.
Friends have gone home.
What's left
is comrades.

If only *these* were not so
remote, righteous, intimate
as gossip in snow.

If they would stop
lying to themselves.
Or if the lies
warmed, were not
wrinkled
and stiff
flapping at the skin.

In such comrades
a comrade could freeze to death,

to death
pushing this brilliant future,
this communism, this human
truth
like a needle that has lost its thread.

ENOUGH!

And now they are no longer
man and father,
woman and mother,
but 2
workers in old age:
heroic and used-up
as smoldering rags.

Her, she's
a tiny cell of light
— 40 watts, say,
against 3 backyards
and one small, dirty sidestreet —
in an immense night.

She dreams no more
than the dog, Toro,
chained to the back porch.

Six days she goes
out in the marbled mist
of streetlamps, dawn, dripping trees,
the sky
with its wisp of moon.

Sundays she sleeps.

Across the city, by the harbor,
the cable coiling
machines she tends
are not what they are,
but the oily roar
of her horizon.
An end.

And him?
Back from the hospital
he sits in the kitchen.
His brain scatters
wishes
and insights, like fireflies
through the terrible spring night

only to say
how dark it is,

how 38 years
boxing chemicals and beakers,
grinding glass,
add up
to $57.60 a month
for life: enough
for dog food, cheap
stupefying wine,
rest beyond belief.

It is more
than enough.

IN THE DECADENCE OF ETERNITY

May 31st, 1978.
Our dwarf star
lolls, still,
over the parked cars, the glass
and chrome, the tar,
the worn naked railroad tracks.

Here, where we live,
workers
are driven into the earth
like spikes. Not gold
but iron,
rust.

They link
age to age,
landscape to landscape,
clay pits
to the brick backs of towns.

And now
the 2 o'clock
train rattles and squeaks
over parched cinders,
easing into the freight yard.

A crew of gandy dancers
in magenta hardhats,
some in undershirts,
some with kerchiefs,
lay down their tools.

They step back
in burning puffs of air
to rest,
it is their right
to rest, still as shepherds
while the grinding wheels pass.

REVOLUTIONARY POETIC

You go
dragging the poem with you.

It doesn't want to.
Has excuses, reasons.
But confused.

How will it squeeze
through, with its
hands in its pockets?
How continue
cultivating tears, airing kisses?
How can it with justice
howl, without
its luminous rage
that never got angry,
that hardly ever
hurt anyone?

And where will it put
the children,
their dew darkened trees,
the pleasant
threat of rain?
How keep
unbroken, unspilt,
the simple glass of water?
Which is. Just is.

And old old innocence
that took
the stick, the cold machinery,
responding only
with morning

with warm steaming milk?
How give *that* up?

Surely it's easier
for a rich man to enter heaven —
than for a poem
to step sinking into revolution,
like Moses
marching into the desert,
making for his promised land.

The poem facing its future
feels like Moses,
the rich man.
When it goes, it can't
even
take itself.

What, then, if it's stuck
paying dues,
magic marking slogans, saying
'this is how it is, and how
it will bo'
and thinking
second thoughts.
Revising, to say
'actually, *this* is how it is.'

What if it goes on
saying and thinking
and is not perfect?

And how, when it goes,
can it keep
kindly, or cynically,
superior?
What if it kills someone?

Worse, what if it doesn't
and is, instead, itself
shredded and pulped?

And if it ends in the dump
with other cadavers
also mutilated,
also scarred,
until even the scars
are stripped from its bones . . . ?
And if, at this landfill
of black plastic bags,
gulls are still
dipping and cresting
over,
like a gale of papers,
and swallows
or whatever they are
darting into the sandbanks . . . ?

Then you just, must,
tell it the truth:
that, well, that's life
and how it goes.
Take it or leave it.

When you go
you don't expect to come out
smelling like a rose.

FRANKIE REYES' POEM

is missing.

Because what's missing
here,
and not only here,
is Frankie's first lesson

(after 32 years put off
he's nervous as a cat
              but
the woman sits him down
with A,B, C, etc.
worrying to bits
a gnawing
sleepless
rat)

because without him
between these lines,
as between the lines
of bilingual
signs in emergency rooms,

here
is a terrible wound

*

Because where are
all, or just one of
his sentimental letters, soul notes,
his pages of roses and moons,
of 'treasure'

where, his playful
machismo
not to be condoned, and yet
where is the gala he is,
the
party wherever he goes

because without this
even
labels on soup cans
are ghastly, tin, stripped
of the simmer and whiff
of cream of asparagus,
of chicken noodle

*

(where is it
the first, unrehearsed
note to his tutor,
a tart
    'X is a brat'
to tease her, but
also to pay her off,
what she has given him
letters for)

*

because *with* this
poems may be poems
not crippled
                precisions,
and leaflets to his life
might not be
bossy, puny

slaps in the face
but speak, eye to eye,
not glazed
not aside

*

Because what's the use
if we can't

(coming
home from work at 1 a.m.
that
night after the first lesson,
scratching away downstairs

at 3 a.m.
wake Sharon up
'Read this read this'
so beside himself
how can she get mad?
'Huh?'
handing her a scrap of paper
'Read this, what
does it
say?'

as she mumbles, mumbling
it
in a daze . . .

and with
Frankie pound the bed
'I thought so!
I thought so!
I thought that's what it said!'

slamming the walls of the
universe, back

like a boy his huge
intelligence
beaming, all
over)

*

because without this without
him
every line,
but especially these,
skips a beat
as it sinks into
something like night

because without him

there is a quibble in the heart
of your joy
and at the heart of your rage
a melodrama

a lie

BONDAGE, BETRAYAL

With so many out of work
the mill town bus stop
puts on
her 14th pot of coffee.
Morning has an air
of afternoons.

Cigarette smoke
crowds
the rack of girlie magazines,
the bondage, betrayal and
child sex books
'for adults only'
at the rear of the store.

What hours of loneliness —
adult
hooded loneliness —
hunch, stand, suckered,
fixated
on power over,
on power over
each own little life,
swaying here in chains of despair

PIZZA

The girl combs combs her hair,
her reflection in the window
practices
tossing its head, *humph*

Older brother on his bed
smokes, floats
upstairs
in bone rumbling stereo

The mother has misplaced
her glasses
or her pocketbook
she walks around looking,
stuck

But the father comes up
dazed from his newspaper,
between Lebanon
and the South Bronx
asks, what's to eat

Ah, that does it

Relieved
they pile into the car,
go for pizza

SANDWICH OF THE DAY

The health food trading post
has just ventured
its 2nd
$10 sandwich of the day —
not without
a sprinkling of 12 celestial herbs
from the ancient wisdom root
under
the fountain of youth —
not without
a sincere, solemn
undulant lecture on Norwegian seaweed

in the bony solitude
of his hands
struggling
to wrap that sandwich.

MOTOWN

The rock star
rising
the hard way,
from an auto workers'
neighborhood in Detroit,
playing the beer halls
the grass and acid alleys
of the Great Lakes,
the Ohio Valley,
singing
the grungy
neighborhood of Detroit

got a smash hit

a gold record

turned this
disc
into a Corvette,
a river cruiser,
a platinum record,
invested this
in shares
of GM,
cashing in
again
on the 1st 2nd 3rd shift
the office drudges
kitchens and kids
of that
neighborhood in Detroit

where his fame
persists,
clings to the street
like confetti
after a wedding,
after the wedding
party has driven off.

WHAT STARTED THIS

fuck you

a young guy
slamming the car door
strides off

from up here I see
her hands turn the pages of a magazine
the head is hidden
one hand flexes stretches
checks itself
the magazine is laid aside
again there are two hands
nerving about in the lonely sunlit car
the hands of a woman
picking at one another for no reason

the car is parked down there
behind the row of stores
by the dumpster
the delivery platforms

looking out there now
we cannot say
what started this

her hand staggering through
the pages of what might have been
a glossy women's magazine

him shouting, out
of love or sex   *fuck you*

but it had nothing to do
with love or sex

IF

capitalism kills

it's not always with a bullet
into a black,
not always a radiated worker
high on grass, packing
an old atomic sub reactor
in concrete, for burial at sea,
not always, even, in boxes of boys
stiff as marines

it kills

naturally, its
murders
are suicides accidents or justifiable
homicides, most don't appear to happen,
even if you aren't laid off for life
cut off
how can you make ends meet
the flat jammed who wouldn't scream
at husband wife kids
one kid yelling down the street
I'm gonna bust that fuckin spic
the girl shy to the point
of torment, scratching at dirt
a third fakes karate
grooves
superhuman concentration

who wouldn't

blow brains out
to alcohol drugs soap operas TV football

music music music motorcycles
quick lays
stereo on the porch, out the window, in boom rattle
rip offs betrayals whiplash comebacks *screw you*

not that there are not
good times too

the car up on cinder blocks
months on end,
working it over with a beer
in the slow close sun of a Saturday afternoon

though no one in the beginning
chose to live this way

no one wanted

to crash racing around
and around, just to get on,
to not to be
rust, used up, over
whelmed by this system
whatever it is
this gelatinous mass murder
this amber where
they are more and more stuck
turning more colorful, sporting
more flagrant heraldic tattoos,
Christ's head on his bicep, the blue
butterfly alighting at her shoulder,
this turmoil where they are
moving yet still
in colorful clothes, colorful language, ever more colorful
freedoms that don't fly,
deaths that hardly ever
got out alive

from this atrocity
where the man beats the woman
breaking glass in the night

this agony, where they are beautiful
yet hurtful to look on
like a live wire, broken crackling and dancing
dangerous in the street
going nowhere

SOCIALIST REALISM

You wonder at
artists, poets, musicians
going off,
praising and mourning
what must be important.

Wonder, too, at what
they pass in silence,
the shuttle and click
click of typewriters
turning to computers, the
humming fluorescent vista
          of women slumped to them —
like perfumed dust rags, ripped off
into smaller and smaller
corners

wonder . . .

I mean, it's
something all that
art that
        gut crashing
flair and risk,
                    priding
laughing talking to itself
weeping
slashing the iridescent murk.
Terrific, too, its gristle and bone
        soaring in darkness
   past
the subsonic bus droning slowing speeding
                                                slowing
                                                            to work

I mean, there must be another way
there must be
there must . . .

TODAY AT NOON THE SECRETARIES
GOT TOGETHER WALKED OUT
& CALLED IN SICK
THEY WON'T TAKE, THEY SAY
ANY MORE OF THIS, THEY
SAY THEY WILL KEEP
ON CALLING IN
UNTIL THEY ARE HEARD

AS FOR THE PETTY BOURGEOISIE

when they herald socialism, democracy and the people
nice and legal

when they rise above the crude questions
of blood and struggle

when they point out oppression or repression
overlooking exploitation

when they rally for every cause on earth
never, though, for workers' rule

when they pronounce workers a sect
and workers' interests sectarian

when even the word, worker, seems to
refer to another species

grotesque, out of style, nearly extinct —
then, surely then, you know their politics

continue their class and its war
by subtler means

KURT R.

Comes home from work
red-eyed
from late night meetings,
alarm lopped sleep,
from all day
sawing sawing pine
studs, glistenings
froze
stiff as bricks.

Stomping
snow from his shoes
he unzips his oversuit,
sprawls in a chair.
Has a cup of coffee.

And basks
in the bright spot
that has made his day.
Banner headlines
in the bourgeois press:
Rockefeller is dead!
Died (official version)
editing a book
on modern art.

Maybe, at last, modern
art has struck back!?

In a pig's ass.
Kurt R. will believe
it when he
sees it.

Meanwhile, considering
his own
bunch of bones
he zips his oversuit
back up,
slowly, as though
stitching up his chest.

He's making sure.
Going
out scattering
Rocky's ashes,
like bright
sawdust on the snow . . .

The ashes
are newspapers
tucked under his arm —
English/Spanish communist
papers he peddles
on West Avenue,
doorstep to doorstep
in subzero weather.

After each stop
he jots down
the number of the house,
how they took it,
why
and why not:

'because it's true'
or, half's in Spanish
or
'it's only a dime'
or
'we don't want that crap . . .'

Cheerful, gaunt, obsessed
puffing and billowing
ashes,
he counts out the change,
now and then
thinking
what are you doing, you sap!
how did you get
into this?

blowing a bit of warm
breath on the littlest finger
of the correct line
a worker must live in this life

WITNESS CÉSAR VALLEJO

We call on
comrade compañero
César Vallejo.

We assemble his
corrections
passions
exasperations,
his nimbus
of humble respects.

To his card carrying
communism we appeal,
his blank passport
utopian
forehead,
his vest and shoes,
his marxist-leninist study groups.
And, why not, his arrogance
his fractured earnestness
so literal!
and the blushing
aureole on his pillar of militant light . . .
Why not!

For his palm pledges
the muscle pump
crammed into his chest.
For, in fact, 40 years dead
and the corpse, which is very dead, is yet
very warm —
like a book, face up
under a single staring lamp!

It has taken dictation,
it translates
oxygen into blood.
But whose, where to? What says
this same comrade
compañero, for whom
the correct line was a spinal column
not a rope or a stick,
for whom the precise path followed
in footsteps
of the Spanish workers' militia,
and through a maze
of International Brigades, carrying
their countries on their backs —
what does he say? this scribe
whose future was as the reptile
left behind, observing
the shoulderly, the modest, the anguished, the firm
pass it by . . .

Who meanwhile gritted teeth
at the wretched, shouted
'Get up!'

And with one nail scribbled
'Do not lie'
and with a painstaking thumb
rumbled
'Trust the workers. Speak with your
production, how much
human you produce,
or shut up.'

Who, having exhausted
this last vein of irony,

breaks off one last
message after the last,
says, simply,
'Serve the sovereign workers.'

At which he begins to sweat bullets
bridges
clouds,
and this and that.
And with his navel
his stunned Peruvian clay
his Parisian rain
he sits down,
cannot go on.
He has forgotten himself.

Now
there is no César Vallejo.

Where César Vallejo was is
the abrupt
erect
million, 100 million, 800 million
corpses of workers —
some angry, some embarrassed,
most plain with wonder
but none, not one, is cold —
who rise now, are rising
laboriously,
sick, and at the same time relieved
to deliver this witness,
and to be
our verdict

WORKERS
UNITED
WILL NEVER BE DEFEATED
OBREROS
UNIDOS
JAMÁS SERÁN VENCIDOS

A militant
unarmed march
to the Brooklyn Navy Yard.

The usual signs,
banners.
Usual chants.
Wave after wave the same

Suddenly
held up: at
the tinkle of glass.
Distant, tiny, shocking
like the death of a toy

Frosted panes
broken
a fist emerged, a forearm
a face, another . . .
In gloom 5 storeys deep
a hand started
waving
from the bottom
of its life,
as a sea fan
rust streaming
ships have passed over

Now
short thick thin leggy
fingers
hook through the window grates:
undocumented workers, illegal
aliens
from South America
Africa
the Caribbean:
shouting
French, Spanish,
tilted and musical English

It is the human rainbow
arrested,
detained.

It had been Bolivian
with Indian cheekbones

It had saved, waited
to cross the Rio Grande
packed in vans
and car trunks
to be shot at,
raped
in the moonless dust

It was Haitians
on rafts
pushing out to sea

landing in these
marine gray
block buildings,
crosshatch fences
raked with barbed wire,

and around these
a field of black
Brooklyn ghetto,

a prison
in a vast
crumbling prison,

becoming this
protest
against this.

Above all it would be
the voice
from a broken window, trailing
down at the end
thonk yooo
thonk yooo

it blew a hole
through everything

from APOLLO HELMET (1983)

APOLLO HELMET

named after
the god of light, music, poetry
prophecy

conceived in the USA becoming
awful
flesh in Iran and other
colonies

is one of the simpler
special tortures

unlike tying one
to a white hot metal table,
unlike his her paralysis,

named for the god
of broad daylight

this has no features

around the victim's head
it amplifies
SCREAMS
10 times what they would be
normally

10 times
normal torture screams

after the god
also of healing
leaving no mark no scar

that's the beauty of it

the essential
message, terror
howls back
louder more familiar
sure we

hear, we heard

even without
this god of poetry
whose name will serve
any filthy thing

the way
scholars and artists
would jet to Persepolis
sucking up
oil
blood money, through
gold plated telephones
in the tent of the Shah:

with
Peter Brook playing
his 'Theatre of Cruelty'
to experts
at the Fifth Arts Festival
of Shiraz, with Ted Hughes
to come through
ORGHAST grunting
among the desert tombs
with Andy Warhol
along with so many others

the stars
whose names
escape us for the moment

along with the light, the music, poetry
the god who serves

torture, murder
you name it
any purpose

name it

NATURE STUDY

Young man in a bathing suit
cool
in July swelter
signing up for the draft

he leans in
on tiptoe, his hidden arm
braced for balance
at the soft worn
edge of the counter,
his other arm
closer

holds out towards the postmaster's window
the form, signed, up over
the heads of scraggly
mostly skinny
surely, in such heat, fetid
protesters sitting and squatting
clogging the way:
too crushingly innocent
to be symbolic,
too idyllic
to scream bloody murder

the young man in the bathing suit
is graceful, courteous,
careful not to trouble them
as they are
not to stop him

it is so dis-
arming, they are
accomplices in
harmony

going off
without a ripple,
the protesters sitting
still, gawking up,
heads tilted
on necks
with the lopsided drift
of lily pads
on pond water

he eases over

dragging no shadow,
no history,
no name for the war
drawing them together

now, in this calm,
as in the eye of a storm

CAPITAL PUNISHMENT

the parents of the dead girl
hang around the prison

they have one question
did he express remorse

she was eight years old
too young for sex
never mind mutilation

did he express remorse

no, no, he went to the chair
"without making a statement"

but did he show remorse

the parents of the dead girl
demand remorse
but quietly

all he ever said was
he did not remember
like nothing had happened

exactly, exactly
that is why
they haunt this prison
its cold stone

they too are children of a sort
they do not want this death

what do they want then

they want
the abomination
of natural justice

the tears of things
blood gushing from the stone

PATHETIC FALLACY

And yet a camera is more
human than a penguin

this doter will ponder
weeks months in rows
the one white egg
balanced
on its broad feet

but the telephone hung up
on a desk
cord dangling
is more
moral immoral

the black and white
bundle
staggers off into spring
unable to fly, flops

tipsy and formal
into a groaning smoking sea,
plunged into

sub-feeling cold
in which
it has no need of us

is this amusing, moving

and yet
a machine a Volkswagen
beetle

a diesel rabbit whose
grandsire may have
been a gas chamber

is more human

WINNING THE MORAL BATTLE

losing the bloody war
the honorable few

advocate passive resistance,
go limp:

the bodies are dragged off
like dead bodies

POVERTY IS A BLOODBATH

therefore we oppose poverty
as we oppose bloodbaths

we are against violence
it solves nothing

we are against poverty
it is hell on earth

against violence we advocate
non-violence,
the antidote to poverty
it's obvious, is money

for the mutual problems
of violence and poverty
this is *right honey*
the solution

a non-violent philosophy
with property and money

THEY GLORIFY NON-VIOLENCE

because the violence is directed
against someone else

because they think the violence is directed
against someone else

because they do not see
how this touches on them

because they do see and are afraid
to call the violence violence

because they can live with it

because they think
they can live with it

because if they name it
they will have to deal with it

because if they name it and don't
do something about it
they will see themselves dismembered

their principles in one room
(at church home school)
their ass in another

because this is how they live,

and if they miss the contradiction
they may watch it on television

pacifists will sit down
under the mantra of non-violence

they will arrange to be arrested
so the violence may go about its business,

because it took violence against
others to make their living for them

took strangers subduing
milking and mining strangers

to refine them, to introduce
sons and daughters into Harvard

it took yet more violence
graphic and distant

a massacre or two on which
to exercise their fine moral anguish

hence they praise it, they

glorify this transparent violence
rather than question or change their life

because this is civilization
as they define it

POETIC DICTION

Certain words are not fit
for poetry.

Boss, for instance.
Our better verse
you may observe
has no boss in it.

The best, in fact
the most refined,
has even eliminated
jobs strikes lock-outs

not to mention unemployment.

Naturally there are no classes.
Rather, no ruling
and no working.
Just, on occasion, a middle
or an English.

It follows there is
no exploitation
no struggle
no poverty
no racist taunts
or murders, and
no injustice

because there is no
justice —

only psychology
begging questions, and
trees, menstrual blood (it's
OK it's animal nature)
with a few obscenities
classical compositions
dewy or sweaty
love, but not often

mystery, fantasy, myth
an insane asylum,
victims without victimizers
as in slabs of veal,
and a little peace . . .

there *is* peace
in poetry, the
pie in the sky
of this vocabulary

which you can bet your bottom
dollar does not include
people with their resilience
their intelligence
seeing through
the culture police.

That is why no one
minds
poetry anymore:

its world is one
nobody lives in, not even
poets who close their eyes
to speak

AGAINST THE WALL

Against the wall
of history
it's Paul de Man

speaking in tongues

upon what rock
is candor to be based

on what rock
enfin do we stand
as we begin to begin
to carry on

if there is none
no rock no
where to stand

speaking in tongues
a voice from the dead

think my dears
candor is baseless
take my word for it

did I say colonize
Jews on an island?
words, just words
without basis

in 1941 or 42
what's the difference
without history
to tell it,
to differ,
to witness to
defer to,
well then

upon what rock
was that island
the Jew island
to be based

none, no one can say,
you will not find it
on any map

spoken in tongues
from the dead

you have my word on it

REVOLVER

Cool to touch, dream
dense   he
was before he
knew it, turning
it over in his hand
oiling the cylinder
spinning it
rapid click hammer
cocked half cocked
ad-
justing trig
ger pressure
painstaking maneuver
reaming, cleaning
the barrel
bluing it, it's
warmer now, sur-
prisingly heavy
loaded

sobering, the
heft of it

he looks up, brushing
aside the litter
the tracts, leaflets, newspapers
novels
slipping it
under shirts socks
pushing shut the drawer

yes yes this
was something solid
in the soft dark,
this was
there under everything

THE LAST SUPPER

ROME (UPI) John Paul II marked
the Last Supper of Christ
and his apostles —
washing and kissing the feet
of a dozen
destitute old men
from a home founded
by Mother Teresa of Calcutta

winner of the 1980
Nobel Peace Prize.

*

John Paul, dressed
in white and gold vestments, holding
the golden staff of
St. Peter, sat
on a velvet throne
head bowed, as two priests
read in Latin and Greek
the gospel, recalling
the last night Christ
spent with his apostles
before his crucifixion.

This gesture of humility
was performed
by the pope, who is also
bishop of Rome,
at a mass in the Basilica
of St. John's in Lateran

where 10,000 people were delighted
by John Paul's joining in
singing
with the Vatican choir.

*

Vatican Radio said
the men were chosen
because they represent
'the poorest of the poor.'

*

Easter ceremonies begin
officially
when the pope lights the large
white and gold candle
by the main altar
in St. Peter's, when

angels who waited
with baited breath, heave
skyward
sighs of relief
as Jesus rises from the dead

as John Paul turns over
all
the riches of the church
to the poor

*

The poor
poor
who were

the sewers
of beds and cribs,
Calcuttas
picked over
yielding prizes
honors, model poorhouses,
miraculous velvet, marble, gold threads
the wealth the church
ripped off

who embodied too
humility
the pope in all
his white and gold power and
glory
expropriated today

kissing and singing

scavenging stripping them clean

THE SOVIET UNION INVADES AFGHANISTAN

When the Soviet Union invades Afghanistan, the Soviet Union invades Afghanistan.

When Israel invades Lebanon, Israel does not invade Lebanon. Israel liberates Lebanon. The operation is called Peace for Galilee.

It takes many corpses to make this peace. Many arms, legs, eyes. Arms to be raised or lowered, legs to crouch running, eyes not to see. And it takes many ceasefires. When the Israelis daily declare a ceasefire, all west Beirut scurries for shelter from the bombs and shells that are sure to follow.

Israel liberates Lebanon from armed Palestinian refugees who live near people. Near Lebanese, who live in the way of Israeli bombs. Even nearer their own families, also in the way. This demonstrates Palestinian cynicism: they wrap themselves in their mothers' skirts. Now, to get at Palestinians armed to protect the refugee camps they and their families live in, the Israelis must shell helpless civilians. Why don't the refugees live somewhere else. Why don't they go home? as a midwestern American reporter put it. Why must they live among people?

On Israeli news, Palestinian refugees are terrorists. Not men women babies, farmers, auto mechanics, secretaries, school kids, girls washing clothes, peddlers, nurses, guerrillas. Including, doubtless, some suicide commando terrorists. No, like any epidemic, homeless Palestinians are without exception international terrorists. That's why the Israeli army must imprison their doctors, cutting off water, electricity, food and medical supplies.

Israel harbors no terrorists. Menachem Begin and Ariel Sharon are not international terrorists. They are Prime Minister and Defense Minister, respectively, of the State of Israel. Yitzhak Shamir is the Foreign Minister. They have not gotten where they are, to become respectable, by blowing up hotels or massacring innocent villagers in Qibya, in Deir Yassin and elsewhere.

This very morning, 4 August 1982, Prime Minister Begin announced, to laughter and clapping from 200 visiting Americans come to support the invasion, that soon he'll be offering package tours of Lebanon, that already at the northern Israeli border there's a tourist boom. "Their hotels are one hundred per cent full," he said. "It should only happen to the Waldorf Astoria." Does this sound like international terrorism? No, it is tourism. He even keeps his word. During the siege of Beirut he sends busloads of tourists to sightsee the new ruins of Sidon

But before tourists arrive in force, Palestinians must be gotten rid of. Naturally it is not enough to kill them. They must be annihilated philosophically as well. As "two-legged beasts." And again, as "drugged roaches in a bottle." So as Begin and Sharon pursue this extermination-and-dispersal policy into Beirut and beyond — not counting Palestinians or goats or shredded orange groves in the death toll, but invoking god the bible and metaphysical genetic superiority over common humanity — their banner of sordid sacred righteousness is raised over the mortified illusions of those innocents who believed fascism had to be German or other, and that victims of racism could not themselves commit racist murder.

For when Israeli soldiers in Sidon methodically beat certain prisoners to death, tying ankles to wrists behind the back and lashing the human bundle to a tree, who was so principled as to ask: if not Nuremburg, where will the war crimes trials be held after *this* war? and who will hold them?

In Tel Aviv 70,000 Israelis with the passionate humane courage of their, our, history protest all this, as Hasidim too hold back, they will not go along, nor will the young Colonel Eli Geva who resigns, and these confirm that history as warm and precious as an arm an eye a leg

yet even these are left behind as events pass them by — as the basket of amputated Lebanese and Palestinian limbs in a basement field hospital under Beirut is also left behind, arms and legs nameless now with no nationality whatever, unable to stop the slaughter, for nothing of this or any historical witness will kick or wave or make anything happen ever again as it looks on, horrified.

But what do they behold? How did they understand what was going on?

For when Begin and Sharon (with their bosses officers and colonial administrators) hired rightwing Moslem goon squads and Christian Phalangist gangs modeled on the Hitler Youth of the 30s, and when they squeezed patriotic anguish and fear from Israeli workers, taxing money iron and blood to pay for this, and shelled not only Palestinian refugee camps but other wretched working neighborhoods, theirs was not the army of a chosen people or a master race nor of the

Jews, but the old pitiless army of class war daily
pounding the rubble of the irrepressible poor

including, in time, the pacifists the socialists the
trade unionists and always at the end of the line,
now momentarily crazed and confused, the darker
impoverished oriental Jews of Israel, too.

For when that army overruns refugee camps and bulldozes
what shelters are left, it wants the homeless
without a country to be homeless without a roof, a
kitchen, a corner to sleep in. It wants those
homeless scattered across the earth, homeless as
flies which it may spray and swat with cluster bombs
and white phosphorus, whose one command is to cut
and burn human flesh.

They do not even eat this flesh. Only destroy, destroy,
destroy: leaving it for anti-semites to feast on,
like maggots, who are the camp followers and secret
agents of General Sharon, Ariel Sharon, the butcher
with the name of god's lioness, of altars, of plains
and Arabian gazelle, who thrusts and lunges from
cabinet meetings to carnage in his body of a
lumbering toad.

And the worst is, the ordinary boyish graying Israeli
soldier is not killing flies. From hills and gun
emplacements around the city, he is pounding and
crushing his speck of a brother, a sister, his
father mother his own children, it is his own death
he is obeying, holding his ears, observing it from a
distance. The silence is sickening

as the quest for a final solution is carried on by those
who endured to prove triumphant there is none. For
what have they sacrificed? To make a homeland

creating endless homelessness. Then why are they closing ranks? To force another diaspora.

Only the names have changed.

FROM THE ASHES

"unabashed
socialist-realism propaganda"
the National Endowment for the Humanities
Chairman called it

funny, I'd thought it
a film about Nicaragua,
about ordinary shantytown Nicaraguans
battered by waves of U.S. marines
yet sprouting up, through
the rubble of Somoza's terror,
growing in patches over the wounds
of this 20th century

still the Humanities Chairman
drew the line, "it is political
propaganda, not the humanities"

and to think I'd thought it
a TV film about a shoemaker
his wife
3 daughters 1 son

actually,
there *was* a newspaper owner
who'd opposed Somoza, and
opposed, now, the Sandinista government
from a lawn chair by his swimming pool:
easygoing, liberal, personable

yet weightless, rattled, his words lost on
the large delicate earthen
shoemaker's wife, learning
revolution from her teen-age daughter

Because of them and many like them
it's true, Somoza had fled
looting the treasury leaving
Managua in ruins

and it's true
the farmers still had it rough,
there they were
right in front of us
complaining to a Sandinista official
things are no better now
than before, and the official
with a pained look saying
"we're a poor country
we can't turn around
overnight it will take years
maybe 10, 20, 30 . . ."
and neither official nor farmer
was content,
never mind happy,
not to have cheaper seeds

maybe that's what the
Chairman of the National Endowment
meant, saying it was
"not the humanities . . .?"

because the shoemaker's wife
was relieved, yet
crying because
under the revolutionary government
all 3 daughters were sent
up into the hills
among volcanos and lakes
to teach the forgotten the peasants
to read and write

she and her husband went
by bus, looking for them
beyond even the telephone,
to make sure they were not
as rumor had it
turning against their parents

in fact the girls were homesick
and wept a little
and were proud, older, also
heavier than before

maybe that's why
the Chairman of the Humanities
attacked this for being
one-sided

because meanwhile Somoza's guardsmen
were in prison,
there, on film,
complaining to the warden
(himself a former prisoner in this
prison Somoza built)
of overcrowding in the cells
because under the Sandinista government
no one was executed
nor tortured,
though early on, out of
rage, grief
and rough justice
there must have been beatings,
and guardsmen in the neighborhoods
who should have been, and were, shot

so the Chairman of the National
Endowment for the Humanities

must have felt
humiliated,
because his own agency had
without knowing it
funded this film

in it
Nicaraguan ex-guardsmen
had joined Cubans in Florida training
to invade Nicaragua
in berets stetsons mirror sunglasses

and an elderly lady
by a palm tree in Managua
was saying let them come, we're ready
they may get in but once here
they'll piss their pants

this in the film
that has undermined the
Endowment for the Humanities

was it that old lady
who did the humanities in?

I don't know, but later
the shoemaker's wife the
mother of 3 daughters
and 1 son, said
quietly half to herself
(or was it her daughter
speaking for her mother?)
before the women just had
washing cooking kids
now she said smiling
there were 'other things'
but did not elaborate

a pity she didn't, she
clearly had news for us

because now life was complex
surprising
the whole family talked together
politics ran a probing unbroken
thread through everything . . .
and when the oldest daughter who
was doubtless the vanguard
and listened to patriotic folksongs
criticized her youngest sister
who tuned in to American rock
the youngest said, wait
you were my age once
you had your time
let me have mine

and the brother mediating
said, look
Nicaraguan music is for listening
American music is for dancing

smiling, pleased

they all smiled, for
that was that

and all this had started
one day
before the revolution, when
the oldest daughter had come home from school
hiding, for the night, a Sandinista flag
and her father had said, why?
we'll all be killed!
but next day walked her back to school
he carrying the flag

because "if they catch us
it's me they'll kill, not you"

now, on top of that

the same shoemaker and his family
who still live in a shack,
these sweet ingenuous people
their plump cheerful daughters
and shy son
have hit
the enemy where he hurts

that they did this, and were
so nice about it,
I mean, that it was
their decency did it,
is wonderful beyond words

because as good as the film
itself makes us feel,
this last
repercussion, which bonds
those people with us
who struck
our common enemy,
and made him pay for it

this was, is, if anything
even more
heartwarming than the film itself

STATE POWER

This is Horace's story.
He says it beats on him
like a bad dream.

Every saturday he passes
leaflets out, at
the mouth of the subway.

He, and a few others.

With a bullhorn
they speak out against
the dictatorship
of bosses.

And every saturday
a gang of hecklers
threatens them.

One fishfaced kid, especially
vicious, gets to him.

Horace knows he could beat
fishface and his buddies
into the ground.

Fishface knows Horace knows,
and Horace knows
fishface knows

because both see
the cop always
there, on the opposite corner,

if Horace makes a move
he'll flash and howl
in a swarm of cops
clubbing Horace to the street.

'So I look at fishface,
he looks at me,
and we both know
what this is all about'

this is Horace speaking.
Which is to say, it is
his gray hair blur,
his round black face,
his candor
and his rage, speaking

it is not a dream.

GOLDEN MEAN

They call the rage of the oppressed
extremist.

Evenhanded
censure,
from the hypothetical center of

the slaughter they call impartial, objective

FAMILIAR TERMS

The senior undersecretary
explains 'hegemony'
in plain terms, to
people like himself:

take Central America. It's
like looking under the bed.
What you find depends on
how far you want to look.

Take Guatemala. It's like
when your neighbor's party
gets out of hand, you call
the police, or the warden
to silence the barking dog
that's keeping you up.

But
what is he talking about?

The party is guerrilla war.
The cops are
the cops, yet are
the father of the girl
picked up for questioning.
They are more the father
two days later in the morgue
stunned, saying 'but
she wasn't pregnant!'

and more, more
the government death squad
that is the father
lifting up the shroud

who sees her belly slit,
stuffed
with the head of her lover

and the senior undersecretary,
the 45 year old teen-ager
incessantly patting his cowlick
is saying: take El Salvador . . .

what is he talking about!?

on the rocks of El Playón
the dog
is already a headless corpse

WHAT IS POETRY

We know it doesn't rhyme much anymore
but is it beautiful is it true
does it transcend the moment
which moment

or is it ironic, does it echo, echo what
does it have ears

at night whom does it adore
yet at dawn
what dream would it go to the wall for

or is it vituperative, why not
doesn't it express powerful feeling,
an overflow of feeling, is it sincere
is that enough

does it lay bare the soul
or explore the give-and-take of intense personal
        interrelationships
which persons, what kinds of interrelationships
work or play or
why one and not the others

is it witty, profound, wittily profound, profoundly witty,
is it avant-garde does it shock the bourgeoisie
who just love it

or is it above the social arena does it circle the earth,
        a satellite with a proper sense of gravity high
        above the winds of fashion
who put it up there
does it transmit breathtaking pictures of a tiny earth
to a tiny earth

if not, is it a vision of eternity
tell us about it

does it make anything happen
or does it die to itself, till others notice the smell
is it shrill does its voice crack
or must it be a baritone of honey
does it give pleasure, does it teach, delight, uplift
whom does it persuade
whom doesn't it

is it a set of rules a code of forms
what is the principle behind the rules
was it handed down and by whom
or pieced together in a workshop too long ago to remember
can it be rearranged on the shelf
who really cares
may it be dismantled

is it moving then, either way moving
is it the imitation of an action
which action

is it a bunch of willy-nilly impressions
who is impressed

if it were a crib
would you trust your baby to sleep in it
bounce up and down in it
learn to stand up in it then
don't answer that

is it a world created by the poet
for the poet of the poet
does it exist for its own sake,
but if it's a way of breathing, whose way

do they smoke are they
breathing making love or getting off work

is it the ideology of a class or the puff of genius
genius for what what class
what are you talking about
is it a man speaking to men
a woman speaking to women
or universal human speaking
to no one in particular
that is, no one at all

is it a mirror held up to nature,
to human nature,
or is it an escape, is it
a mirror held up to nature, to escape human nature, or
a mirror held up to human nature
to escape human history

are you afraid of it
do you understand it

does it embody human values,
values as they are
or as they say they are,
which humans, which values
is it for or against
or does it take no position,
where did it go then
does it levitate, is it in heaven

is it then beyond all this
what is it, where, if you know tell us

but if you don't know
shut up, we'll understand

AUTO-DA-FE

Confess
to buried rage

to reading and teaching
dumb books
no one could get through

confess
to professing
autonomous genres,
blindsided
histories of silence

the stupefaction
of culture
mugging the poor,
the filthy lucre
of museums and concert halls
rolling across the marble floor
like the small change of schoolchildren
who pay for this

*

confess

you too subscribed
to the mute
articles of this faith

therefore we burn

POE VOTES

Wednesday Oct. 3rd, 1849
all liquored up
and dragged
(Crane guesses)
retching through Baltimore,
polling place to polling place
to Ryan's 4th Ward,
each time a different
dead man, with
his semblance of a life,
and each time
under another name
this same sad man
dying those deaths
became
a whole gang of votes:
this sorry man
jingle man,
this haunting
genius of American letters

FLAMING A

1

his was a flame
no hand could contain

his pure anarchy
his black flag trailing smoke
desolating our enemies

he was an inspiration
to us all

2

the hand came round
in back
through his art, his career, his shoulder blades
his ambition
to serve the people

it came round stroking him

3

the body politic
wearing its glitter suit
swallowed him whole —
it gulped him down
like an old carnival sword swallower
a fire eater
eating fire and sword

4

he still doesn't know
(in the dark he calls freedom)
within whose bowels
he rages

THE SHAMEFUL DREAM

the house was burning

in the morning we woke up
everything was usual

except the wet
electrical stink
like an iron on an ironing board

each night
into morning we dreamed
the same acrid odor
the same feeling of disbelief

one morning leaving
we looked up

the roof had caved in
the attic lay open
like a window in springtime
the pent-up must of memories
was airing out

rafters were poking about
smoldering O so discreetly,
wisps of gray finer than hairs
curled off the charred timbers

everywhere
nails stuck out, useless

the light pouring down was brutal

everything up there
in the shameful dream
had blackened to a soft blur

and it was steaming,
burning off the dew

THE SACK OF POETRY

We were saying
we wanted to be the flag
the flame

a clarion call
clear as water
this would not be

poetry it would not
stand out
from anything else

but in the book
of the German poet
we found those very words

with their flags
their flame
the exact same words

they were claiming
victory in the field
the sack of poetry

I was speechless

"OUR GOD, OUR HELP IN AGES PAST"

When hymns were still
dangerous unscriptural
Isaac Watts the Dissenter
was writing hymns

hymns to God
against the government

against the Church of England
its rituals its schools
the authority
vested in its powers

he composed for children
for pious souls
"even of the meanest capacity"

for the poor powerless
who could not read nor
graduate, ever, into
the ministry of death

yes, he took *Psalm 90*
out of the Old Testament
abolished the wrath of its God
absolved its men of death
of dying because
they were children of men —
meaning in Old Testament
gender, human

but no no no, death

death was the sole property
of "tribes" and of "nations"
whose sure end
he predicted again and again

nations were flowers
withering into the dark
tribes were the dreams
that die at daybreak

now these many years later
in what Watts might be
pleased to call darkness
the dream nations
sing this hymn at church
they can read the words
they read them
to express general piety

and having generalized
the piety
they take it to war with them

they take it to the university
in textbooks
anthologies of poetry
the words without their music

where it is boring

hey but
hold on, you say
you want to say
it is not boring
it is heroic, defiant

it speaks for dissenters
in another language
like the one we speak
but not, alas, the one we speak

whereupon the student
waxing poetic in the spring
of final exams
writes in the wan pulp of his bluebook

So has the original intent of the poem
been borne away by the tides of time.
Now, instead of seeing a piece of
literature confronting a burning issue,
we see just another poem.

It is left to us
to make of this what we will

TKO

In his heart of hearts
his deep dark
metaphysical concept

he concluded
the time had come
and gone

bam! out
like a light,
a halo of black stars . . .

yet even as
he dwelt on this
the time kept

coming and going
coming and going

back of his neck
he felt this,
yet did not dare

admit it, not
to himself
not to anyone

WHAT ARE WE WAITING FOR

We are waiting for the moment
to make our move

as we did in
fact, in one or another
capital, under dusty palm trees, wait out
splintered bursts of gunfire,
the body of naked rags
bunched-up at a snag in the river

yet this too passed

oranges tumbled into market bins
bottles of milk were stacked in the shade
all by themselves
the children took a bus crosstown to school
someone disappeared
we had another cup of coffee
3 days later we heard
he had been picked up about the time
the kids were coming home from school

what could we have waited for
a solar eclipse? declaration of war?
what was so unusual?
it was just another day

now gone.
                    You eat
an apple, work out, have
a glass of beer, water the cactus
once in awhile
read a book, vow

to be honest and straightforward
hedging only a little

cheating only
on death, taxes, beauty and, sometimes,
the harder truths

but in how many days
who will tell you
nothing was as it seemed, say
who has been taken away
or maybe a job
possibly yours, or
everyone's Social Security

and that the world we see
we live in
does not (never did) exist

RHODODENDRON

for Arlene

You said, there's a poem in that rhododendron.
I said, not for me.
Elizabeth Bishop, maybe, but she's dead:
tough-minded lady with her cigarette always
smoking, I liked her, we both did,
though she *did* make that racist
sexist remark
about cigar rollers in Tampa.
The words out of her mouth
left her propped at the podium
like a quaint, raspy doll.
I almost felt sorry for her.
She had become a period piece.

Yet to her credit, in its heyday
the flat skeptical voice kept damping down
the pollen dust she kept stirring up.
She picked and praised, yet
with a few colorful exceptions
hardly ever got carried away or lost
in the bug-eyed, detailed, luminous rush
where time broke off

where there was a poem
in the rhododendron.

*

But what I meant was not
what Brecht meant, either, asking
what times are these when
talking about trees is almost a crime,

because such talk is so much silence
about so much horror.

How could it be criminal
to speak of trees!

I meant: the horror, or what
that cloud of a word covers up,
has come over
the look in the rhododendron,
has left only
this fleshy leaved bush
of big beautiful flowers

but where's the poetry in that?
where is Elizabeth?

*

(what I remember is
the bright snappy day
the genoa sails popping out
fantastic blues, oranges, reds, slippery greens
leaning and skipping like berserk bloomers

we were flying a kite out over
the shallow scallop waters off Duxbury
hauling, tugging
before the line broke

though the kite was so far away
by then, when the twine
dragging like cable, parted, surprised

we didn't mind, in a way
we were relieved, giddy,

Elizabeth fluttered a little
and was, clearly, pleased)

*

one day we're caught looking

bumblebees and brass-jacketed flies
poke about heaps
of milk pink fluff

as though the yard were 13 or 14 years old
again, beside itself with its first
floppy corsage

the rhododendron grew so fast!

blossom to blossom
blew, crushed

we're puzzling now the odd
petal in each cluster,
the yellowish thumb smudge
of darker yellower spots

we are watching the sun
grow quietly old

*

trees have something to tell us
we could not tell ourselves

*

Ar, I do thrill to some poems
I mean, the honest that open up
looking right at us,
opening *us* up,
I enjoy the rhododendrons
the pink more than the purple,
they're so fresh
they will never be accomplices,
it's not that I can't feel for this
or for Elizabeth or what
made Brecht cold as leather,
doesn't it get to most people?

but if there's a poem in this
it will have to be
you, saying
(don't ever stop saying it)
there's a poem in the rhododendron

(insist, insist) there's a
poem in it!

CULTURE WAR

"The gods of China are always Chinese."
— *Wallace Stevens*

I no longer write poetry. Which makes this a chastening prospect — like an out-of-body experience in which you hover over the past, vision fogged, trying to make sense out of the someone-or-other feeling its way back there. What did it think it was doing? I'm not sure. Even then, while still writing, I did not consider myself a poet. That was a chafing honorific, like the proverbial Sunday suit on a farmer. Writing poetry was something you did. What you *were* was more complex than that.

At 19 I attempted my first poem. Thanks to open admissions, with no money or certifiable qualifications I walked into a local college and signed on. It was a way to avoid fulltime work and to put off active duty in the Navy. One day during a March blizzard I wrote a poem for a composition class. Aside from the usual suspects of an English Lit Survey, the one poet I knew was Bobby Burns. His poems, the only ones in the house, belonged to a Scottish uncle who rented the room next to mine. So I wrote a satiric Scots dialect poem on a Saint Patrick's Day parade. The teacher was enthusiastic — the piece won the school's poetry prize — and that was it. I had begun writing.

I look out over this selection and I have to ask, who wrote these? Really. Where do the poems come from? The question is not what the poetry is about — a dumbed-down, dead-end question — but what is it doing. I showed up at that college with a squareback duck's-ass haircut and 13" peg pants with velvet stripes inlaid down the sides. From here I find it almost moving — it is beyond ridiculous, it is unimaginable — such a person showing up at the admissions office of a one-building, raw brick teacher's college. What may be difficult to appreciate, for anyone in a position to read this, are the radical disjunctures of a hood coming in off the street: turning up where people 'naturally' go to college, read literature, conceive careers. I had not seen the inside of an art museum . . . and wouldn't, until years later, when in Rome on a fellowship. I could dance and play basketball, but was inarticulate in this bemusing new world where I sat down mystified before table settings with *two* forks. Mostly I watched, listened, and had the good fortune to be adopted by some teachers, bohemians, and Korean War vets in college under the G.I. Bill. The vets, themselves double-edged and streetlike, not only helped in the transition but shielded me from i.d. checks at jazz clubs. The bohemians were passionate misfits: independent women, undercover (not closet) queers, working class intellectuals and foreigners, people who had no cultural place or who did not submit to the one allotted them. This was in 1955, when the bohemians around commuter colleges had a different trajectory than the middle-class kids from elite colleges who tended, then as now, to make up countercultural 'movements.' We had no comparable quarrel with so-called high culture. For many of us it was a novelty, and we had no qualms about rooting in its fissures. As for the teachers in that place, they had a remarkable contempt for academic bureaucracy — not only waiving course requirements, but making me leave their school for a more challenging one, and they made the arrangements! I left there with wild misconceptions about the fluidity and freedom of academic environments.

Encouraged, I imitated poetries and intonations, exercising through dictionaries of poetic forms in much the same way as I watched to see which fork to use. Eventually I realized that metre isn't marching orders — that the kick, the sensuousness of prescribed verse comes from counterpointing the speaking voice over against expectations raised by the metrical scheme, and from the cross-cutting syncopation of line breaks. Poetry ceased to be an acculturation process and became something truly engaging: a kind of thoughtful body english, like jazz, in which you had always to keep your wits about you.

Up to that time, no one in my family had finished high school. There had been no need to. Nor had we any notion of 'culture' as a distinct social category. (It's easy to forget that the rolling canon of graphics, writings and musics called culture is a sublimation of middle-class, specifically bourgeois, perspectives vetted by academic and other social-management institutions. Culture in this valorized, controlled sense does not exist among working class people as such.) Poetry then, as a function of culture, seemed to be written in a provisional language — for me, a second language — that was never wholly *present*. Despite the sensuousness of poetic movement, there was an air of unreality about it. It was something from an other world. That was one oddity. Another is that I did not have the career ambition that runs incessantly through the hopes and fears of middle class life. It's embarrassing to admit, it seems so naive, but I never intended to get anywhere. I had no image, no concept even, of a future. But not being black or a woman, and coming along during the fifteen or so years when US hegemony was on a roll, I lucked out . . . went Scot free, like an indentured servant melting away into the landscape of colonial Georgia. And that was where the novelty wore off. I'd come into a world of amenities, a world that dreams it privileges thinking, but where arrogance and class complacency are stupefying, like a gas that no one smells. A person would have to stumble into it from outside, as I did, to appreciate the devastation. To this day it amazes me. I have never gotten used to it. There was lots of wonderful stuff out there, some of it called poetry . . . but what should have been a humanizing vista of self-recognition was being trivialized, systematically trashed, with classbound status- and style-mongering. Meanwhile the specific gravity of reality, as I understood reality, remained back there somewhere, in the strata of people who are largely beneath notice, or who are muted objects, in the middle-class-contained poetry version of life. My street and gang combativeness was rekindled then, with some confusion, into social indignation.

I wish I could say the indignation was clean burning, but it was not. Roving street reflexes had carried over into the high motives. I could write calm but not calmly — could write cool, rather — but in my pulse I was as wired as a junkyard dog. Still, that edginess was nothing new. The more profound problem, as regards a dignity-offended poetry, was that I had to write it in a second language. Using poems to wage this particular culture war was like going to battle in golfing duds. Career indifference had freed me to take positions I might not have taken had I been fearful or concerned to get ahead, or had I felt that middle class cultural terms corresponded to 'reality,' which I did not, yet that very freedom was also the catch! Middle class culture seemed little more than a code, an elaborately institutionalized figure of speech. Even so, that culture held the only poetry game in town. My own poetry, though defining itself in struggle against classbound culture, nonetheless remained a function of it. I had to speak what I felt and believed in a language sphere I could not wholly credit. In time this bind became a preoccupation. The poems would turn, fixated, on poetry itself, which came to resemble not a flying horse but a snake-infested head. I was stuck.

The giddiness of first publication, which was sudden and deceptively easy, had come in the early 60s. My poetry teacher had taught me to associate writing integrity with graceful writing — so that, whatever their common obscurities, my poetry was always cleaner and more transparent than the prose. After the first little whisks of publishing dust had settled, however, I stalled. Calculation, and knowing how to write, were not enough. It took stretches of doldrums before I realized I could write only if and when the rhythm, the configuration, felt inevitable — if, and when, the poetry wrote itself. Still later, after Chile (1973-74), I would have no interest in writing out of personal compulsion, or not that alone, but only when the writing was *socially* called-for. Having managed to slip through a crack in the class system that determines 'culture,' feeling I'd half gotten away with something, I was obliged to speak with consciousness of — though I could no longer speak with *the* consciousness of — those who are not so much silenced as wadded-up and discarded out of mind. Not that my reversion happened all at once. Obsessed with technique, or what passes for technique, for awhile there I went along and fit in. It was almost that simple.

Sometime in the mid to late 60s I stopped 'making poems' and began to *speak*. Unlikely as it may seem, the signature drugs of the period barely touched me. The rush was in the social upheaval, in going hand-to-hand with events. Life and thought were exhilarating, stressful, productive and up for grabs. There was a poignance to this, as in a second youth — or in a second chance at a more socially-redeeming youth than the first one had been — when you throw yourself into projects you know will hit the wall. What gave hope, gave not just an air but a touch of reality, was that black and white working class kids were still finding a way into public universities. Unlike now, it was assumed that they counted, even if only as a nuisance to be put down, placated or distracted. No one was beneath notice.

I was writing AVENUE OF THE AMERICAS (1971) — actually the less-than-mythic Sixth Avenue where my friend Grandin Conover worked at *The Nation*. Some of the poems are acts of bravado. That the bravado is wholehearted does not entirely excuse it. Other poems are speeches addressed to silences, specifically social silence, because that is where US poetry was most evasive, especially about its own class determinations. I myself lost touch in a different way. The nagging aestheticism of AVENUE keeps hedging what had started out, brashly and idealistically, as a struggle against the fetishization of poetry. The aestheticism comes through not in what the poems say but in how they carry themselves. This is especially true of the letter poems exchanged with Grandin, who committed suicide in 1969. Our presumption was to take poetry as seriously as we took life, with an innocence hardly imaginable now. Innocence not as ignorance, but something flat-eyed and intrepid. We were not children. We *knew* what was going down.

There was more to the aestheticizing, however, and the more was Yeats, who was already a period piece. His bardic gestures and rhythms stepped out like aging marching bands, as did his politics, which I either ignored or was too apocalyptic to notice. But Yeats' posture, his audacity, was something else. The person who said he had not given a penny for poetic airs unless he believed the poet had a sword upstairs — that figure was compelling. For us, living our own period piece, it was unthinkable not to back up our saying. Which is, I suppose, just a retro-macho way of declaring that whatever poetry is, or what we thought it was, it was not fiction.

Between THE MARCHES (1967) and AVENUE I began to use elaborate, less accessible metres adapted from Greek and Latin. They provided a discreet lifeline as I felt my way toward a looser-jointed verse. Much of the metrical 'quoting' came from Horace. The bonus was that his letter poems showed how to speak matter-of-factly while accommodating disparate realizations, pretty much as in life. *Shall I make sense or shall I tell the truth?* asks the breaking-down woman in "Seele Im Raum," a poem by Randall Jarrell. T'ang letter poems provided another model, as did Coleridge's suppressed "Dejection" letter. This is common now, but at that time poems tended to be organized situationally, thematically, laid out in litany or catalog, or huddled under the umbrella of a trope. The Beats had disconcerted some of that, as did later so-called Confessional poets, but always from a self-centering basis, as an elite. They aspired to be heroic, not in martial terms but via a radically redefined notion of heroism . . . a highly contagious disease, as I can attest. As far as contemporaries were concerned, the more promising US poetry models were certain black poets — Mari Evans and Carolyn M. Rodgers come to mind — because they dealt from where they were, not from where the overriding culture presumed they should be, and dealt *as* they were, not as 'best minds' or other prodigies. They were not beyond their history.

Still struggling with the problem of a second language, I became aggressively idiomatic. Mouthing did not so much replace hand writing as accredit it. If a line or phrase couldn't be spoken, it didn't fly. This was due more to circumstance than to principle. As the 60s cut across campuses and streets, I found myself giving speeches. With all the pressures and conflicts there was almost no way to shut up. The turn toward idiomatic language, then, was less a function of realism or integrity than an expression of anger. Often the speeches were analytical attacks on the institution I worked for. I was disenchanted by liberalism, in fact stunned by it, specifically as it dissociates belief from conduct. Not that dissociation is avoidable, but it seemed intellectually and morally offensive that this condition should be a source of pride and principle . . . that one could know what must be done, yet fear and despise the doing. It interests me to see, now, how doggedly the poetry keeps coming back to this *impasse*.

In 1973 supported by a fellowship, intending to emigrate, I and my family went to Chile. We were en route in Mexico when the Allende government was overthrown, Allende murdered, and the military junta installed under General Pinochet. We stayed in Santiago for nearly a year. SANTIAGO POEMS (1975) is anomalous in that it carries over the liberalism of earlier work but does so only as a cover. Although involved in organized resistance to the junta, I had to write as though we were spectators. My wife, Arlene, and I had been approached by the MIR (Movement of the Revolutionary Left), a guerrilla organization. Our apartment became a safe house. We also did recruiting and helped with mundane chores. The MIR had checked us out by taking AVENUE OF THE AMERICAS for analysis. Our contact, who spoke no English, returned a few days later. Speaking by rote, he reported their findings: "A little bit hippie, a little bit left, a little bit Trotskyist." Then he turned and smiled. "But very definitely left." If in some painted heaven there's a circle for charming, efficient reviewers, ones as mischievously innocent as *putti,* surely this MIRista should have a place in it.

Except for one secretive piece occasioned by a recruiting fiasco ("Guerrilla"), nothing we actually did showed up in the poetry. Not that there was anything romantic in the doing. It wasn't even as though we chose to be involved. There was no choice. As with many of our late 1930s generation — growing up through WWII and its aftermath with the larger-than-life consciousness of kids — the worst thing to be was 'a good German,' and the worst thing to do was 'pull down the shades.' To not see, that was the horror. And if you did not act on what you saw, how could you live with yourself. It was not enough merely to 'witness.' So you were stuck with that ethic — if you were not cynical, that is, and took to heart the highminded stuff being pumped out with increasing intensity after the war.

I stress this because there are many ways to misread the situation, especially for those who haven't lived this history, and because SANTIAGO POEMS was left to hover over its own realities. I'd have preferred to speak from the nerve-racking maze of actual resistance, a situation that English-language poetry does not get into, but even later that was not possible: we continued to have friends in Chile, and then the Pinochet regime lasted so very long. The general is still, to this day, commander of the army. What's curious is that I don't recall the Chilean experience as a horrific one, perhaps because there was no trivia in it. The least look or phrase mattered. Even so the experience must have been terrifying, it exacted such discretion from the poetry. The changes in our life and outlook could not show up until we returned from Chile in the aftermath of Nixon, Watergate and the Vietnam War, and then those changes would appear, in the poetry, not as reportage but as a redrawn politic.

SCRAP BOOK (1977) reflects the turmoil of political transitions both before and after Chile. From it I would have to conclude that the clearer the politics are, the less revved-up the voice will (have to) be. The analytical edge of "Innocence," a gloss on Merleau-Ponty's *Humanism And Terror,* frees that poem from the more rhetorical forms of irony I had had to rely on in AVENUE. But in this eclectic book I was also working on more problematic strategems. "Seize The Day" tries to demystify *carpe diem* by lumpenizing it, treating the genre as a sort of emperor's new clothes, but it was also supposed to document a phase of my youth, if that's the word for something so exhilarated and unfeeling. None of this made the poem less offensive, of course, especially as it lacks any shred of fictive morality. To make matters worse, by the time of writing the poem I had come to *feel for* its feeling-impaired youth. The poem was too mimetic a messenger of some very bad news. And then the genre critique didn't come through. Difficult as it is to attribute literariness to a document of social pathology, it's even harder in the academic environments that host the preservers and discussants of poetry, because there the fear of unboxed thinking — really, anxiety at the prospect of losing control — only reifies the going canon of mental categories. Provocative socio-literary issues not only don't get discussed, they don't even get to exist as categories. Finally, the title of SCRAP BOOK was intended to shrug off this collection of occasional pieces and experiments that couldn't go anywhere anyway because there was no critical community in which they might be tempered or developed. Besides, Chile had already turned the poetry away from self-referential literary questions. I didn't stop thinking about them, but for some time I no longer dealt with such issues through the poetry, turning instead to essays.

The real Santiago book is MAY DAY (1980). On returning to the US I joined a Marxist-Leninist Party, convinced that without a class analysis — or whatever sees past oppression, which is symptomatic, into the exploitation that makes oppression necessary — what we see is shadow play. I learned then that US poetry may on rare occasions tolerate the raising of class issues, but only if these are presented as issues of race or of Third World victimage. That consideration influenced MAY DAY, which nonetheless tries to render people who do not exist in the heartland of US poetry, notably people in struggle. I have to admit also that in "Cold Rags" there is a hint as to why, after five years, I left the organization, which had become a stickler for remembering everything except why it existed in the first place.

A word about party language. Liberal academics tend to object to Marxist-Leninist slogans on the grounds that they are crude, simplistic, and violent . . . the cultural equivalent of nasty, brutish and short. Yet liberal culture is itself propped with simplistic, wrongheaded slogans, such as that asserting the autonomy of art. The difference is that they're not recognized as such. Slogans, of course, are everywhere. Civic space is unthinkable without them. My problem was not with slogans, nor with the violence of party language. Why take offense at violent language when the language of non-violence, of peacemaker missiles and democratic imperialisms, of the purity of arms, is a rancid anthem of exploitations, oppressions, wars and other murders? The problem, for me, was that the party's slogans pressed on like stripped gears. Having projected themselves into a ritualized, symbolic language — a language posted like commandments at the end of time, where none of us lives at the moment — these particular Marxist-Leninists, unlike their prototypes, did not mean what they said. They were more considered in their practice than in their speech, which was grindingly heroic. Clearly they knew better. It was as though they felt guilty about using a language commensurate with their limited, imperfect, worthwhile actions. For that and other reasons spilling over from party macho and dishonesty, I left. So MAY DAY is both a party and an anti-party book. But what then? Having associated poetry with social struggle, I had to keep *doing* or stop writing.

It was difficult, like blowing a wheel on the highway. How do you keep going? I couldn't stop to watch the traffic. That is, even if I could, I couldn't. I had, and have, a deep distrust of spectatorial writing. Not that hands-on experience guarantees knowledge. In Chile we not only worked with the MIR but sat among palm trees and flowers in the park, and passed by the few paintings in the museum, while around us, where and when we did not happen to look and see, people were disappearing. People we *knew.* Imprisonment and torture were the happening, not palms or paintings. But then you can't know anything simply by 'being there' anyway — not even by coming across a body in the river, or glimpsing the interior shadows of men crouched against the frosted glass panels of an ambulance. Even when it is generated on the scene, your interpretation cannot account for, cannot *hold,* its objects. A certain humility is in order.

"The plum survives its poems," said Stevens, a realist. W C Williams thought poems should not interpret reality but render it intact, "as grapes are round and come in bunches." Maybe. But words are not their things. You can rub words against words until you're blue in the face, getting neither light nor heat. In the end it is imperative to *take on* what is out there. There is no poetry on museum walls, only trophies. The single recourse is to plunge struggling into the totality of whatever this is we live in — not play safe by framing bits of local color, or settling like lint into deep dark psycho-emotional pockets. This is not a matter of program, programs are an issue of time and place, but of attitude. I'm reminded of Mao's injunction that to know reality you must change it. "If you want to know the taste of a pear, you must change the pear by eating it yourself." But of course this is not about plums or grapes or pears. It's not that simple. With us there is always that amazed knot of self-consciousness. There's no getting away from it. Meanwhile, off the museum wall the face of poetry changes. A sign of life! It starts to show its age.

In APOLLO HELMET (1983) I went after 'poetry,' trying to separate the ripe from the rotten but also, and really, just looking for some other poetry to talk to. But whose? With a few exceptions there was little comfort or light in US protest poetry, which lacked camaraderie. At least the poetry lacked it, not so much the poets, or not those for whom struggle set the rhythm of their lives. In life, even with the contentiousness, class struggle tends to *socialize* those who are engaged in it. Within the singular ideological sphere of 'culture,' however, struggle isolates. Dissenting poetry would be fitful, dispersed, at rare moments admirable, and strained, like monologues in a wilderness. You were expected to come to it bearing grains of salt. So I turned toward certain Europeans, mostly in middle and eastern Europe, looking for where the romance, the mythification, the righteousness and self-intoxication of 'poetry' had been wrung out. I wanted something without gibber or evasion, a poetic language that did not posture or veer off into mealy inconsequence — something like the poetry of Rózewicz or Erich Fried, tempered poets for whom poetry seemed to be not a career but a struggle. For what, I'm not sure. A specifically human existence, I like to think. Their poetry was civilized, personable and humane in a way that politically struggling English-language poetry was not allowed to be because no one was listening to it, not even its yea-sayers and allies. Somehow I was left writing poems about poetry. That was the gist of APOLLO HELMET, whose title poem is about a torture instrument with poetic resonance. Is there an irony of ironies? Is it anything like a holy of holies? I hope not.

Years ago in Santiago I wrote a poem for Isabel Letelier — whose husband Orlando, a minister under Allende, was in a concentration camp on an island in the south of Chile. Neruda had scratched some lines to her on a napkin, which was among papers the soldiers had confiscated when they took her husband away. I wrote "Isa Mar" in lieu of the lost Neruda lines, and to celebrate the richness of the space left by her imprisoned husband. About a year later he was released and flown to exile in Venezuela. One night, back in the US, I received a call from Caracas. It was Orlando, thanking me for the poem. I was shocked. Sobered, really. I knew then, as before I had only felt, though felt deeply, that poetry too can be real. Some months later Orlando was assassinated by a car bomb in Washington DC. I tried to write to that, but except for a single phrase botched the job. As I said, it is not always possible to be a poet. It is rarely possible. Stevens called poetry "a violence from within that protects us from the violence without." Well, it is and isn't, it does and it doesn't. Poetry is not a magic amulet. It is something that some people do, but do so differently, sometimes so remotely, you have to wonder if you and they are living in the same world.

The culturally unspeakable fact, and it surprises me even to think it, is that what this conflicted history is about is what Caliban is about. That may be why, I now notice, traces of an untransfigured frog prince turn up in pieces as far apart as "Facing Up" and "Guerrilla." Of course it is not Caliban but Ariel who is almost always associated with poetry — Ariel, the reluctant yet obedient cultural enforcer who spies, provokes, produces lulling strains and engages in something much like torture. Caliban is considered a subhuman made dangerous by his acquisition of a specifically human technology: language. Incredibly, he's no happier with the situation than anyone else is!

> You taught me language; and my profit on't
> Is, I know how to curse.

You taught me language . . . But whose problem is this? Is he an ingrate? Is that the truth of the matter, or simply one of its facts? He is not insensible. He does hear, opening up to, "sounds and sweet airs."

> Sometimes a thousand twangling instruments
> Will hum about mine ears; and sometime voices,
> That, if I then had wak'd after long sleep,
> Will make me sleep again: and then, in dreaming,
> The clouds methought would open, and show riches
> Ready to drop upon me; that, when I wak'd,
> I cried to dream again.

The problem, or should I say the trouble, with Caliban is that he is not impervious: he doesn't make the right *kind* of sense. He does not know his place. Worse, he's passionate about it. About his reality. I have to confess that when I consider what he stands for — and what the 'profit' on the language of this culture is — I feel a sadness and an anger I could not begin to put into words. There is a tragedy of Caliban, a social not a personal tragedy, but the culture we conceive is not wide enough or deep enough to realize it.

Recently I've begun writing plays. Or learning to. Not that theatre is less classbound than poetry — if anything it's more so, being hogtied by the economics of the business — but it does admit to a greater range of social realities. Of course the fundamental exclusions remain: culture as we know it is not democratic and does not aspire to be. An oligarchic mustiness still clings to it. Despite the considerable redirection brought about by two women in movement, and despite tentative 'ethnic' openings, the poetry institution and its politic may be more classbound now than it was 25 years ago, when 'poetry' also meant voices speaking from the heart of black, and occasionally white, working class life. Lacking the mass political movement that made an opening for those voices, the least we can do now is insist on democratizing the *concept* of culture — pressing the recognition that, no matter how glossed over it may be, culture itself is a symptom and a site of profound social struggle.

James Scully
20.VI.94

NOTES

AVENUE OF THE AMERICAS. “Dead Letter” and “Avenue of the Americas” were part of a letter exchange with Grandin Conover, a playwright and poet, who committed suicide in 1969. The verse letters were published in a chapbook, *Communications* (1970). Conover had two plays produced: *As The Hawk Sees It* (Chicago, 1962), and *The Party on Greenwich Avenue* at the Cherry Lane Theatre (New York, 1967). His poems were published posthumously in *Ten Years* (University of Massachusetts Press, 1972).

SANTIAGO POEMS. "Mummies" was a pre-*golpe* term for rightists, considered by leftists to be a kind of living dead.

APOLLO HELMET. “Apollo Helmet.” Apollo is the god of poetry. The Apollo Helmet was a torture instrument used by the Shah of Iran's police. The helmet, a cylindrical affair, amplified the victim's screams *to* the victim. The Shah would sponsor jet set arts festivals among the ruins of the ancient city of Persepolis. This particular festival was attended by artistic luminaries such as those named in the title poem. ORGHAST, by Ted Hughes, was reportedly a "pre-language" (*sic*) version of OEDIPUS.

Many of the previously uncollected poems are from WORDS WITHOUT MUSIC, an unpublished chapbook. “Our God, Our Help In Ages Past” is a hymn by Isaac Watts (1674-1748), the Dissenting minister who set the standard for English hymn-making.

SELECTED BIBLIOGRAPHY

Poetry

THE MARCHES, Holt, Rinehart & Winston, 1967
COMMUNICATIONS, with Grandin Conover. Edited by Robert Bagg. Issued as Poetry Signature #6 by *Massachusetts Review,* 1970
AVENUE OF THE AMERICAS, University of Massachusetts Press, 1971
SANTIAGO POEMS, Curbstone Press, 1975
SCRAP BOOK, Ziesing Brothers, 1977
MAY DAY, Minnesota Review Press, 1980
APOLLO HELMET, Curbstone Press, 1983

Translations

PROMETHEUS BOUND, by Aeschylus. Co-translated with C.J. Herington, Oxford University Press, 1975.
QUECHUA PEOPLES POETRY, co-translated with Maria A. Proser, Curbstone Press, 1977
DE REPENTE/ALL OF A SUDDEN, by Teresa de Jesús. Co-translated with Maria A. Proser and Arlene Scully, Curbstone Press, 1979
POETRY & MILITANCY IN LATIN AMERICA, by Roque Dalton. Co-translated with Arlene Scully. Afterword. Curbstone Press, 1981

Anthology

MODERN POETICS, ed. McGraw-Hill, 1965. Revised edition: MODERN POETS ON MODERN POETRY, ed. William Collins, Ltd., 1966

Essays

LINE BREAK: POETRY AS SOCIAL PRACTICE, Bay Press, 1988

James Scully lives in San Francisco.